SECRETS OF DISCIPLINE

12 Keys

for raising responsible children

Ronald G. Morrish

Woodstream Publishing
Fonthill, Ontario, Canada

U.S. Edition

Copyright © 1998 by Ronald G. Morrish

Illustrated by John Boon, Welland, ON, Canada

Cover design and associated graphics by
Joanne McNay, Port Colborne, ON, Canada

Computer graphics used by permission of SoftKey Multimedia

ISBN 0-9681131-0-9

Woodstream Publishing
P.O. Box 1093, Fonthill, Ontario, Canada L0S 1E0

Publisher's Cataloguing-in-Publication Data

"Secrets of Discipline: 12 Keys for raising responsible children"
Ronald G. Morrish

Woodstream Publishing, Fonthill, Ontario, Canada

ISBN 0-9681131-0-9

1. Discipline of children. 2. Parenting 3. Teaching
4. Raising children 5. Classroom management

Printed in Canada by Lincoln Graphics, St. Catharines, Ontario

To all the dedicated parents who have invested untold time and energy in an effort to raise responsible children....

And to my own children, Terry, Darcy, Alexander and Suzanne, who prove every day that the investment is worthwhile.

Table of Contents

Part 3: Teach Skills

Part 4: Manage Choices

Part I

Discipline Gone Awry

Feeling Frustrated?

Are you tired of bargaining with your children just to get a little co-operation? Are you frustrated by their lack of respect? If so, then you are not alone. Millions of parents and teachers share your concerns. They have watched children become more aggressive and are worried about the lack of safety in our schools and communities. They have seen the disruption in school classrooms and are worried about the quality of education. They have witnessed the lack of respect in children and are worried about the future.

What has happened to discipline? Could television and the movies have such a negative impact on our children? Many people think so. Others believe that social issues are to blame, including poverty, abuse and the breakdown of the family unit. Research says that every one of these concerns plays a significant role. That's not a surprise.

The only real surprise is that no one is investigating the most obvious source of problems. As you will soon see, many of the problems with discipline lie within discipline itself. Many of the strategies that we presently use to raise our children will not give us the kind of children we want.

Everyone agrees that we must raise our children to be responsible and co-operative. This is the only way that we can have confidence in the future of our communities. Unfortunately, today's popular discipline will never accomplish this task. It actually encourages children to become manipulative and non-compliant. It teaches them to play life like a chess match, move and counter move. Parents and teachers are forced to make deals with children and threaten punishment just to get a few chores done and have rules obeyed.

It doesn't take long for adults to become so exasperated and frustrated that they feel like giving up.

Now, don't misunderstand. This doesn't mean that it's impossible to raise responsible children using today's popular discipline. After all, there are a lot of great children in the world. Obviously, some parents and teachers succeed - but it's not easy. Even at the best of times, discipline is exhausting and everyone has days when they wonder if it's all worthwhile. Fortunately, many of these problems can be avoided and that's what this book is all about.

The first step is to understand what today's popular discipline is all about. You see, discipline keeps changing. It reflects changes in our society. During the past 40 years, discipline has gone through several dramatic transformations.

Remember When?

Until the 1960's, discipline and obedience were considered virtually synonymous. The goal of discipline was to instill in each child a form of respect for authority that would result in the child following adult directions without question. Children were to "be seen and not heard". Any form of disagreement with adult direction was labelled "talking back" and was dealt with accordingly.

> *Then we became concerned that children were overly submissive and lacked independence. As teenagers, they felt obligated to rebel against adult domination and the abuse of power. We realized that discipline had to change, so....*

Into the 1970's, we followed the advice of psychologists who suggested that children should not be inhibited. Parents were supposed to unconditionally give and give to their children, demanding little in the way of chores and responsibilities. They weren't to use the word "No" because it could lower a child's self-esteem. Rudeness, anger and defiance were to be viewed as healthy outlets for hostility and accepted as a natural part of growing up.

> *Then we became concerned that children were turning into spoiled brats who thought that the world should revolve around their personal rights and needs. We realized that discipline had to change, so....*

We adopted the principles of behavior modification. We learned to reinforce desirable behaviors with praise and rewards. Undesirable behaviors were to be reduced or eliminated through the use of negative consequences, usually scolding or the removal of privileges. Consistency was considered a key factor in determining the success or failure of our efforts.

> *Then we became concerned that we were conditioning our children like we were conditioning our dogs. We felt that behavior modification was cold and impersonal. We realized that discipline had to change, so...*

...we moved toward today's popular discipline.

In the 80's and 90's, freedom of choice became the major social issue and constant demands were made for greater personal rights and freedoms. Child advocates argued that children should have many of the same rights and should be allowed to make more of their own choices. Supposedly, this extra freedom would prepare children for life in the modern, rapidly-changing world.

Proponents were convinced that children would learn to be responsible by experiencing the consequences of their choices. The role of adults would be to encourage good choices and discourage poor ones using the rewards and consequences they had learned for behavior modification.

This new system was referred to as "behavior management".
It is the system that almost every parent and teacher uses today. Open any of today's books on discipline and you will likely be reading about these techniques.

Come Again?

Don't worry if you find these last two stages a bit confusing. Many people do. So, before going on, let's clarify the difference between the old system called behavior modification and the new one called behavior management. With behavior modification, adults told children what to do and rewarded them for complying with the instructions. With behavior management, children are given the freedom to make their own choices and are rewarded for making good ones. Just remember the word "choices" and you will have the central theme of today's popular discipline.

The problem is that somewhere along the way, we forgot to limit children to the choices that are their's to make.

Children, granted the freedom to make their own choices, are far too liable to choose irresponsible and antisocial behavior. Many parents and teachers are now worried about the breakdown in respect for authority. They are concerned about increasing disruption in school classrooms and about the lack of safety in our schools and communities.

As you read the "Secrets of Discipline" you will understand how discipline has allowed these problems to develop. You will see that today's discipline fails to teach children the skills they need to become responsible, co-operative and productive. It also promotes a value system that is opposite to what you want to see in your children.

Some Children are Bound to Struggle

You will also understand why this system of discipline fails certain children. Impulsive children, for instance, rarely benefit from behavior management. This is one of the reasons that children labelled ADD (Attention Deficit Disorder) seem to be "coming out of the woodwork" these days. Children from dysfunctional and neglectful homes are also likely to struggle. The same is true for underachievers. For all these children, behavior management fails to teach them the skills and attitudes required for success in the modern world. Could it be time, once again, for discipline to change?

Choices, Choices Everywhere

Today's world is a "think-for-yourself" world. Our children hear it all the time. "Think for yourself. Think for yourself." Children are expected to make their own decisions and learn by experiencing the outcomes of their actions.

The Belief

is that children will learn from their experiences and will grow up to be responsible, co-operative and productive.

Most parents and teachers have adopted this approach. The result is that children have found themselves surrounded by choices. At home, many children are allowed to decide what to wear, how to do their hair, what to eat and when to go to bed. Their bedrooms are often treated as private areas and neatness is a personal concern.

The school environment is much the same. Children select their own activities. Line-ups are passé. Clothing is a personal statement and dress codes may be considered an infringement of individual rights. Students have even been given the freedom to decide on the quality of their work and the marks that they wish to earn.

Teachers readily adopted behavior management, not just because it was recommended by experts, but also because it fit well with other educational theories. During the 80's, about the same time as behavior management came on the scene, educators embraced the "discovery approach" to learning. This approach was based on the premise that children learned concepts best if they discovered them on their own. Entire programs were redesigned to allow children to select their own activities. Techniques such as direct instruction and lecturing fell into disrepute. Educational goals emphasized the need to develop "independent, self-motivated and self-directed learners".

As a result, it was natural for teachers to adopt a similar approach to discipline. Behavior management is, in effect, the discovery approach to discipline.

But Wait!

Will this approach really teach children to be responsible? Should discipline be designed so that children will learn life's important lessons from their own experiences? Consider this true story that formed the basis for a television documentary. Not only does it provide great insight, its ending is a real surprise.

Khaled had spent his life herding camels across the deserts of Saudi Arabia and Egypt. He had no formal education. His father had been a camel herder and his grandfather before him. Everything he needed to know had been passed down from generation to generation.

The camel drive was difficult. Even though the camels were stubborn and temperamental, they had to be kept moving. Otherwise, the herders would be

attacked by bandits who lay in wait in the desert. Move too fast, however, and the camels would lose weight which would lower their value at the market in Cairo.

There were also large areas of shale which had to be crossed. The camels' feet had to be protected with leather "shoes" or else they would go lame. Since lame camels would slow down the drive and make everyone an easy target for the bandits, they would have to be destroyed. That would upset the owners and the herders would lose their pay.

On the last night of the drive, everyone was sitting around a fire discussing the problems that had occurred on the journey. The commentator turned towards Khaled and said, "I want you to know that I'm really impressed with everything you've learned from experience." Khaled leaned back and laughed. "We have an old saying", he replied.

"It's the unlucky who learn from experience. The lucky learn from the experience of others."

That's right, and this is what discipline is all about. It isn't supposed to be a system where adults allow children to learn from their own experience. Real discipline is the exact opposite. It's a system that adults use to *protect* children from life's painful experiences. We want children to learn from *our* mistakes and the mistakes of others.

We already know that drugs are addictive.
We've seen the tragic results when people drink and drive.
We know the life-long impact of dropping out of school.

Our children shouldn't have to learn these lessons for themselves. They should learn them from us. The discovery approach may be good for playtime, kindergarten and computers. When it comes to raising children, however:

> ### *Discipline cannot be done by the discovery approach.*

It's time to get discipline back on track. We need real discipline in our homes, schools and communities. We need discipline that teaches our children the skills, attitudes and knowledge they so desperately need in order to live in the modern world. Behavior management will never do the job because it lacks two of the three critical components of real discipline.

The Building Blocks of Discipline

Real discipline has three parts and they work like building blocks. Each has an essential role to play in creating the structure that we call discipline.

One component focuses on training children to comply with rules, limits and adult direction. The second focuses on teaching children the skills of being responsible and co-operative. The third deals with the management of choices, which is the part presently covered by behavior management. The training and teaching components form the foundation for discipline.

Now that you know what the three parts of discipline are, it's time to take a closer look.

First comes the "Training" part of discipline. In their early years, children are impulsive and self-centred. They want their needs met immediately and hate to be denied anything. Just think of them as having a natural form of "Centre of the Universe Syndrome".

If these behaviors were allowed to continue, then children would experience all sorts of problems during their adult life. To avoid this, we have to teach them to obey adult direction, to respect authority and to comply with rules and limits.

This part of discipline raises a lot of eyebrows. We live in a world which stresses individual rights and freedoms and people wonder if it is appropriate to teach obedience to children. Not only is it appropriate, it is essential.

Every one of us must be willing to comply with certain rules and limits, whether it be for driving cars or respecting another person's property. This is the structure which allows people to live and work together in families and in communities. It allows everyone to feel safe and secure. Either people buy into this structure or they buy into chaos.

The second building block of discipline involves the teaching of skills. The only way that children become responsible and co-operative is to learn the skills associated with these attributes.

They must learn how to resolve conflict, how to work and play with others, and how to set personal goals. They must learn how to organize tasks and manage time. They also have to learn the important skill of self-discipline so they will be ready for independence. After all, we won't always be with them to govern their choices and decisions. They have to learn how to do it for themselves.

These skills aren't learned by accident. No child masters the complex skill of responsibility merely by experiencing the outcomes of personal choices. Instead, these skills must be systematically taught using appropriate teaching techniques, including direct instruction, practice, correction and review.

In addition, parents and teachers must require children to use these skills in their everyday interactions. This takes patience and determination. Skills develop over many years and continue to grow right through adulthood. Learning never stops.

The third building block of discipline deals with choices. If children are to become responsible adults, they need to be given more freedom as they get older. This is where they make many of their own choices and learn from personal experience. Adults provide the guidance that children require so they learn how to take the rights and needs of others into account.

If you think this sounds a lot like today's popular discipline, you're right. The management of childrens' choices is what "behavior management" is all about. It's an essential part of discipline because it provides our children with opportunities to develop independence.

This is good news because it means that you don't have to drop all your present strategies. Over the years, you have probably developed a good deal of expertise about behavior management and the use of rewards and consequences. You also know all about giving choices to children. Hang on to these skills. They are valuable.

All you need to do is improve your skills for the other two parts of discipline. You won't find this difficult because you regularly use these skills in other facets of your life. You just didn't realize that they apply to discipline as well.

The Missing Triplets

Today's popular discipline does a good job when it comes to the management of children's choices. Unfortunately, that's all it does. (Hence the name "behavior management".) The training and teaching parts of discipline are missing.

Where children require limits, behavior management substitutes choices.

This lack of limits has an extraordinary impact on our children. The problems created by this system are the focus of the next few chapters.

Behavior management also has no teaching component.

Children are expected to learn their skills from personal experience. Supposedly, they will learn to be responsible and co-operative just by experiencing the outcomes of their choices.

This is why so many children are struggling these days and why so many adults are frustrated with discipline. Behavior management doesn't work because it gives children choices without laying the foundation. First, children need to be well-trained and well-taught. Then, they are capable of handling their choices with maturity and sensitivity.

 *Remember that children who are not well-trained and well-taught are often called "unmanageable".*

That's right. If you don't do the training and the teaching parts of discipline, then the management part won't work for you.

So when you think of discipline, think of all three parts. Train your children to comply with limits. Teach them the skills of being responsible and co-operative. Then, with this foundation in place, gradually increase their choices so they learn to handle independence with responsibility and maturity.

3

Where Have All The Limits Gone?

Would you give children permission to fight? Would you allow them to be rude and inconsiderate? What about failing in school? Is that a choice they should be allowed to make? Well, if you think this could never happen, that no one would be so foolish....

Think again!

Believe it or not, this is precisely what happens when you use today's popular discipline.

That's because behavior management substitutes choices for limits.

To understand how this happens, listen to the way people speak. When you learned behavior management, you learned the language of choices. You learned to speak in "If...then..." sentences. You hear them everywhere you go; in the supermarket, at school, in restaurants and at shopping malls.

"If you don't settle down, then we're going home."

"If you behave, you can have a cookie."

"If you talk that way to me again, you'll go to your room."

"If you fight, you will go to the principal's office."

Let's take a close look at this last statement. These days, people everywhere are trying to establish limits on violence. They want children to be less aggressive on school playgrounds, at home and in the community. However, this rule will never do the job that people want it to do because it does not set a limit. It does not restrict fighting.

Remember that all "If...then..." statements are choices. What this rule actually says is,

> "If you don't mind going to the principal's office,
> then fighting is one of the choices that you get to make
> at this school to solve your problems!"

If you don't believe this, think about professional ice hockey. The rules state that if you fight, you will get a five-minute penalty. Now, do you believe that this rule means fighting is not allowed in professional ice hockey? Obviously not.

What this rule really says is, "If you don't mind taking a five-minute penalty, then fighting is one of the choices that you get to make to try to win the game." It's a choice and the players treat it that way. Here is the typical thinking pattern:

> "Well, let me see. If I can sucker the other person into a five minute penalty as well, or if we're far enough ahead or far enough behind that a couple of goals won't matter, or if I can take out one of their best players, then fighting might be a good choice."

For an even better example, imagine yourself on the ice. You are the last person on defence and somebody's going to skate past you for a breakaway. The rule says if you trip him, you will get a two-minute penalty. What should you do?

The coach has taught every player that, in professional hockey, you can "kill off" a two-minute penalty 83 percent of the time, but you can only stop a breakaway 51 percent of the time. It's clearly worth tripping him and if you don't, you will be in the coach's doghouse so fast, your head will spin. After all, the rule doesn't say not to trip him; it says if you trip him, you will get a two-minute penalty.

This illustrates one of the major flaws of behavior management. You've been told that rewards are positive and children want them. Similarly, you've been told that consequences (or punishments) are negative, and children avoid them.

But that's wrong.

Because in hockey, if an opposing player is going to get a breakaway, taking a two-minute penalty for tripping him is called....

"taking a good penalty"

....and many of our children understand this concept intuitively.

Now you understand what often happens every time you direct your children to do something. They stand there and mull things over, just like the hockey player. They weigh the advantages and disadvantages and then do whatever is best for themselves, even if it's wrong.

To help you avoid this problem, here is the first secret of discipline:

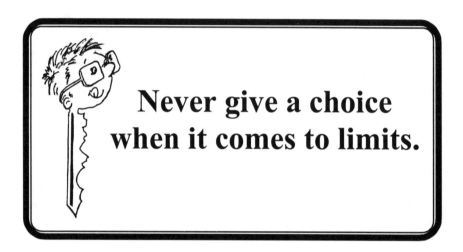

Never give a choice when it comes to limits.

Whenever you set limits and rules, state them in a way that leaves no doubt in the minds of your children. The old saying is, "No ifs, ands, or buts!" You have to speak like this:

"No fighting!"

"That's rude. We don't speak that way in our home (or school)."

"Walk."

"Finish your homework."

No deals, no bargaining, no pleading, no convincing.
Just limits.

This is particularly important in schools where teachers must deal with large groups of students. "Conduct Codes" should be written in such a way that students will know their limits.

"At this school, fighting is not permitted."

Or...

"No fighting."

Of course, there is more to limits than simply writing them into the Conduct Codes. Teachers must also speak to children this way every single day. All those "If...then..." statements should only be used when discussing the choices that really do belong to children.

Beating The System

et your thoughts go back to the game of hockey. Because the rules are presented as choices, most players and coaches consider fighting and tripping to be "part of the game". The goal is to win and it's a real challenge. Many of the most successful players are the ones who learn how to beat the system. They learn how to "get away" with a great deal of grabbing, hooking and tripping. They also learn how to "sucker" the other team into taking penalties.

As you have seen, today's discipline presents rules and limits in the same way that hockey does. As a result, many children see discipline as a game - a game that they feel challenged to win. Just like their hockey heroes, they learn how to beat the system. To do this, children learn certain skills and develop certain traits. The more skilled they become, the more they will be able to "do their own thing".

Here are the most common traits. As you read them, you will find yourself thinking about certain children, probably the ones who cause you the most headaches.

The Balk

If parents and teachers are willing to bargain for compliance, then it's worth waiting to see what's offered. Children quickly learn "the balk". When instructed to do something, they stall, waiting to see what will happen. They make comments like:

"I don't want to."

"This is boring."

"Do I have to?."

They want adults to negotiate, to bargain for compliance. Once children know exactly what might happen in the way of rewards and consequences, then they decide if the task is worth their effort. If they're lucky, the adult will decide that the job isn't worth a hassle and will do it on their own.

These are the children who constantly test you to see if you will follow through. They want to get more and more while giving less and less.

Immunity

The quickest way to defeat the behavior management system is to develop an immunity to consequences.

"So, send me to my room. I don't care!"

"So what if I can't go outside today. I didn't feel like it anyway!"

"So, give me an F on my work. Marks don't count."

Some children even become immune to praise. John finally hands in a completed assignment and the teacher praises his effort with, "Good job, John!" John replies, "Yeah, well. I could have done better."

Once kids master the "I don't care" attitude, then you don't have a handle on them anymore. You lose all your power. This is why adults become angry when confronted with the "I don't care" attitude.

The Sneak

The next skill that children learn is to become sneaky. They spend a great deal of time and energy scanning for supervision because it pays to know where adults are at all times. Then, whenever no one is watching, they can "do their own thing". They don't have to worry about getting caught.

In school, these children always know when the teacher's back is turned or the teacher is busy with someone else. They know who's walking past them in case it's someone they can trip, poke or make a provocative comment to, just to get things going.

At home, you start talking on the phone and,

...just like magic,

...the kids start misbehaving.

Sometimes it seems that children must have six-foot-long antennae that alert them to the opportunities to misbehave. This shouldn't be a surprise, though. After all, today's popular discipline teaches them to do what is advantageous. It is only natural that they would learn how to take advantage of certain situations. It's great fun to be out on your own in the community, to wander down to the washroom at school, and to be left alone in a shopping mall. One can only imagine all the possibilities.

"Not Me!"

Many children learn to shift responsibility away from themselves. Suspected of misconduct, they automatically deny any involvement. When confronted, they challenge adults to find proof. Only when overwhelming proof has been obtained will they finally admit to any wrongdoing. By then, adults are usually so worn down that they merely give the old lecture, "Wouldn't that have been easier if you had told the truth in the first place?"

What is amazing isn't that children do this, but that adults consistently fall for it. Many times, adults will actually witness a child's misbehavior and still make the mistake of asking that fatal question, "Did I just see you hit him?" The child quickly answers "No" and the game begins.

There are other very effective ways of deflecting responsibility. Many children learn to make excuses for their behavior. They blame others for their problems or play the role of the victim. They claim that everybody picks on them. Nobody listens. Life is unfair.

The Reversal

The trait that children are developing faster than any other is "The Reversal". Many children have learned the behavior management system so well that they are now able to reverse it, using consequences to manage and regulate adult behavior. When kids don't get what they want from adults, they have temper tantrums, yell and slam doors. They behave in ways that embarrass parents. At school, students disrupt lessons

and some even throw furniture in an effort to discourage teacher demands.

Now, children are learning the subtle art of ignoring. They not only pretend that they didn't hear your instructions, they sometimes act as if you don't exist. Have you noticed how effectively they tune you out?

The Intimidator

Some children, as they become older, learn to use intimidation as a means of managing adult behavior. Provocative language becomes common. Their "body language" is aggressive and confrontational. Clothing, boots and "accessories" convey the same message. Always, there is the threat of unpredictable aggression.

Faced with this intimidating behavior, most adults become passive. They avoid making any demands for fear of upsetting the teenagers and provoking retaliation. Parents stop enforcing rules. Teachers allow work to remain unfinished. Everyone avoids the areas where these teenagers hang out. Gradually, adults become cautious about their own behavior for fear of upsetting these teenagers and provoking retaliation.

When Did Everything Become a Deal?

The more that children develop these traits, the more adults are placed in a real bind. Somehow, limits and rules have to be enforced, but how? Here is where many parents and teachers begin to walk down a very slippery path. Worried about losing control, they increase their use of rewards and consequences. In effect, they do more of what didn't work in the first place.

Better rewards and harsher consequences usually work for a short time. This is because children play along to see how far this deal-making will go. Before long, however, they become just as resistant as ever. When you play this game, the children always win. Never try to out-manipulate a manipulator.

To improve your skills with discipline, avoid being caught in this trap. Always remember the second secret of discipline:

If you bargain for compliance now, you'll beg for it later.

Bargaining is a trap. Sooner or later, you will find yourself offering rewards that are completely unreasonable. You will probably start by paying money for chores. Then, you may offer money for good grades in school. By the time your children are teenagers, you may find yourself offering the really big rewards - a television set for keeping the bedroom clean or a car for graduation. (If you don't believe this, just wait till you read the letter to Ann Landers in chapter six.)

At the same time, you will find yourself using bigger and bigger consequences. If "grounding" a child for one night doesn't work, maybe a weekend will get the message across. Before long, the child is grounded for weeks, or even months, at a time.

When penalties and punishments go this far, children begin to lose the very things that make each day worthwhile. It is not unusual to hear of children whose birthday parties have been cancelled as a punishment for their misconduct.

The clearest example of just how far this deal-making can go, and how wrong it can become, occurs in many institutions which deal with difficult children. It has now become commonplace for such institutions to require children to earn points in order to buy the "privilege" of going home on weekends.

This is how desperate adults are becoming as they try to design systems that will convince children to obey rules and directions. Visiting one's family is not a privilege. It's a basic need. No one has the right to use a family's love and devotion as a manipulative device. So, be careful. It's very, very easy to fall into this trap.

Here's the Clincher

By now, you may agree that
discipline is way off track.
If not, then this will convince you.

Be forewarned!

Today's discipline may teach your children a value system that is completely different from what you want.

**You want your children
to know right from wrong.**

**Today's discipline teaches them
to do what is advantageous.**

This is how rewards and consequences work. Children weigh the advantages and disadvantages of their actions and then make their choices. They do whatever is best for themselves.

This value system leads directly to another problem that is equally serious. Today's discipline teaches children a completely different, and very narrow, view of responsibility.

**When your children make decisions,
you want them to take the rights
and needs of others into account.**

**With today's discipline,
kids base their decisions
solely upon their willingness
to live with the consequences of their actions.**

With this system, children feel empowered to do whatever they like, as long as they are willing to take the punishment. The obvious problem is that there are lots of children who are willing to take any punishment that adults are prepared to use. They know we don't want to use corporal punishment any more. They know the juvenile court system will probably only give them probation for the first few charges.

When we teach children this value system, it's just like giving them a licence to misbehave.

Worried About the Teenage Years?

Have you heard all the cynical comments about how difficult it is to live with teenagers? Don't believe it. There are lots of great teenagers in the world. It's certainly reasonable to expect some friction along the way as the teenagers develop their sense of individuality. This is an important and natural part of growing into adulthood. We can live with that.

What we can't live with are teenagers who have a completely different value system than we do. As they push for independence, they do things that are offensive to parents and teachers alike. They do whatever they want with little regard for the rights and needs of others. When it comes to penalties and consequences, teenagers invariably believe that they can handle anything that comes their way.

This is why it's so vitally important to lay a good foundation when children are young. Real discipline is a lot more than simply giving choices to children and then dealing with the aftermath. We have to teach them right and wrong. We have to teach them to respect legitimate authority. We have to teach them the lessons that have been learned by others and by ourselves. Then, and only then, will we enjoy watching them develop into adults.

On The Endangered List

When we talk about the endangered list, we are usually discussing animals. These are animals for whom the world has become a hostile environment which doesn't meet their needs. As a result, they are in trouble and need our assistance. This is no less true of children who are forced to live in a hostile world without the tools that are supposed to be provided for them through discipline. These children are in danger as well and must fight hard just to survive.

It is already clear that today's popular discipline does not help children who learn to defeat the system. They become manipulative and irresponsible. Many are destined for trouble, particularly during their teenage years. Imagine the difficulties of going through this stage with little regard for rules and a great desire to get your own way, regardless of the consequences.

> But these are just the children who **acquire an immunity** to consequences, who learn how to throw up an "I don't care" attitude. What will we do with all the children who have a **natural immunity** to consequences because of the pain and turmoil in their daily lives?

These children genuinely don't care about the rewards and consequences that adults give out because they hurt so much already.

Maybe they're neglected, or their family is breaking up, or their parents drink and fight, or a grandparent just died. The list goes on and on. Discipline fails these children because it relies on them to do something that they are incapable of doing. It relies on them to care. When it comes to consequences, we have to understand that there is nothing we can do to some children that is worse than what life is already doing. Unfortunately, the persistent use of punishment may serve to reinforce their view of life as a painful experience.

Are there other children who don't care and who would be immune to today's discipline? You bet! Count in any teenager whose hormones are running. They only care about one thing and it isn't rules. Any attempt to use consequences with them is likely to produce a sullen, unco-operative attitude or outright defiance. Sometimes it feels like they've forgotten everything that we ever taught them.

Then there are the teenagers who drink or do drugs. Once the "high" starts, they are blind to the possible consequences of their actions. Depressed children are another group. Their emotions are numbed by their illness. They don't care about anything or anyone, including themselves. It doesn't matter how much adults bribe or threaten, it won't help. Rewards only cheer them for a moment, if at all, and consequences drive them deeper into their depression.

Now Reflect on This

Behavior management not only requires children to care, it also requires them to reflect. This is the skill whereby people consider the outcomes of their actions and choices. They judge whether their choices were appropriate and successful. Did they take the rights and needs of others into account? Would they do the same thing again or choose a different course of action?

For rewards and consequences to work, children have to recall what happened to them when they were in certain situations and use that knowledge to change their behavior the next time they find themselves in a similar situation. Impulsive children struggle with this task. It is even more difficult for children who are severe enough to be diagnosed with Attention Deficit Disorder (ADD).

By definition, impulsive children act before they think. How are they supposed to learn from a system of discipline that requires them to think for themselves? That is their handicap. It is precisely the skill they do not have (and may never completely develop). Is it any wonder that impulsive children are becoming more obvious in our schools these days?

For an ADD child, a think-for-yourself world is a dangerous world. The moment the child's brain goes into gear, impulsivity rules. Mistakes are inevitable along with the punishment that invariably follows. ADD children need structure. A substantial portion of each day must be governed by routines which limit the need for them to think about choices and make decisions. For them, an unstructured day is a recipe for disaster.

> For all these children, today's discipline fails to provide them with the structure that they need to be successful in the modern world. We have to do better. It's not just for the children. It's for all of us.

Dear Ann

Now that you have a good understanding of the problems caused by today's discipline, let's see how they look in everyday life. The best example that I have seen of these difficulties was in a letter written to Ann Landers by a frustrated and exasperated parent. Every parent and teacher finds it easy to identify with the situation described by "Wigged Out".

Throughout this letter, you will see all the strategies that we discussed in previous chapters. You will see the threats of punishment, the deal-making and the ignoring which form the basis for today's discipline. As one strategy after another fails, you will hear a parent ready to give up.

Dear Ann Landers,

I am a single parent who works full time. I have two bright and talented daughters, ages 14 and 12. They share a bedroom that looks like a cyclone hit it.

I am tired of yelling at them to straighten up the room. Their clothes are on the floor, on doorknobs,

everywhere. The beds are never made. Papers that are two weeks old are strewn all over, along with soft drink cans, orange peels, you name it. They look so neat and nice when they go out, no one would suspect that their room is a pig sty.

I've announced that I will not buy them another piece of clothing until they learn how to take care of the things that they have. I have also threatened to stop their allowance. They couldn't care less. I even tried an incentive, offering to redecorate the room with new furniture, comforters, sheets, etc. Still no action.

One day, I decided to quit fussing and see how long it took for them to get tired of it. It didn't work. Their clothes literally covered every inch of floor. You couldn't tell what color the carpet was. It didn't bother them in the least. They just walked over everything and went on with their routine.

I don't think I'm asking for too much, Ann. Do you? Please tell me what else I can do before I go crazy.

(Wigged-Out Mom)

If you share this parent's frustration and understand how she could be driven to write this letter, wait until you read the answer. Then you can also share her sense of real helplessness.

Dear Wigged Out:

You can't do a thing about the slobs, but you CAN do something about yourself.

Shut the door of the pig sty and vow never to go in there until they leave for college, marriage or a career, whichever comes first. Tell them where the sheets and pillowcases are and inform them that they can get fresh ones if and when they want to. The same goes for the towels.

My plan may not get them to clean up their room, but it will reduce your blood pressure and promote peace, which is more important than an orderly room.

(Permission for reprinting granted by Ann Landers and Creators Syndicate)

It's important to understand that there is no criticism of Ann Landers here. "Wigged Out" would receive the same answer from most other behavior "experts" simply because this is the answer that goes with today's discipline.

Before proceeding, let's be clear on the real issue that has "Wigged Out" so frustrated. Contrary to how it first appears, this letter is not about the cleanliness of the girls' bedroom. Nor is it about a child's need for privacy.

If you don't mind a messy bedroom, if you want to allow your children to have their own space, that's up to you. These are decisions that parents can make for themselves. However, if cleanliness and organization are important to you and you instruct your children to clean their bedroom, then they should go and do the job. Parents have the responsibility to make these decisions; children to accept and implement them.

That is the real issue here. This letter isn't about the state of the bedroom. This letter is about compliance - are the girls going to follow parental instructions or not. In the case of "Wigged Out", she tried everything she could think of and the girls refused to do what they were told to do. She wrote for advice and was essentially told to give up.

This is the position that discipline has put us in by allowing children to make choices that are not theirs to make. Forced to rely on rewards and consequences, we feel obliged to overlook the open defiance of children who won't buy into our system. We end up feeling helpless. This system could just as easily be called,

"Kids will be kids" discipline.

This is what everybody says, "Kids will be kids". There is nothing you can do to change them. After all, they have free will, right? So all you can do is change yourself.

Well, if Mom gives up now and simply shuts the door, what will she do when this defiance escalates? If her daughters decide to skip school, stay out past curfew, and break house rules about booze and drugs, will she ignore that, too? Will she just shrug her shoulders and say, "There's nothing I can do. Kids will be kids"?

Parents who allow their children to be defiant on "small" issues should be prepared for years of grief. Defiance doesn't go away. It grows in leaps and bounds. This is the start of a long and painful journey.

This is not the path that parents and teachers want to go down. Children need to learn respect for parental instructions and rules. They also need to learn respect for their teachers and other people in legitimate positions of authority. Bargaining and threatening won't do this job. Nor will ignoring.

Fortunately, there is a better way. Read on.

Part II

TRAIN Compliance

To Think
or
Not To Think!

When parents and teachers use rewards and consequences to get compliance, they are treating compliance as a thinking issue. This is why children so frequently respond to our directions with, "Why should I? I don't want to! What do I get if I do it? What will happen if I don't?" They want all this information so they can decide on the best course of action.

Often, we respond to all these questions by having a discussion, trying to convince them with logic and reason. We ask them to recognize the importance of responsibilities and to consider the feelings and needs of other people. We might even ask how they would feel if the roles were reversed. Children are supposed to think about the possible outcomes of their behavior and make good choices.

This is *not* how basic compliance works.

Let's look at the most compliance oriented task in the world - driving a car. When you go out in your car, you are certain to arrive at intersections that are governed by stop lights. If the lights are red, you stop.

Why?

Why do you comply with the rule about red lights? You may think that it's for safety reasons, but it's not. Safety was the reason the stoplight was put there in the first place, but that's not why you stop. Neither do you stop because you think about all the horrible things that might happen if you don't. Actually, your mind is probably elsewhere. You could be thinking about work or trying to remember the items you were supposed to buy on the way home.

The reason you stop at red lights is because you always stop at red lights....
It's a *habit*.

Compliance with fundamental rules is a **non-thinking** activity, the exact opposite of what is created by today's popular discipline. Actions which must occur with certainty cannot be left to the discretion of individuals. As soon as people start to "mull over" rules and directions, many of them will either act impulsively or will decide to do whatever is advantageous. Training people to respond habitually to certain situations avoids these problems. Many of the rules and laws which govern daily life work this way.

You wouldn't enjoy driving in a world where everybody who gets to a red light thinks about whether to stop or not. There are countries where they drive this way and it's crazy!

This isn't to say that all compliance works this way. Lots of rules are thinking rules. 'Yield' signs for instance require a driver to use personal judgment. The important issue is to understand which rules are which. When rules are designed to govern fighting on a school playground, no one should rely on the personal judgment of students. Children have to be trained to obey foundation rules without question and without discussion. That's the way it is in the adult world and that's the way it should be in the world of children.

Learning from the Best

So how is this accomplished? Let's look at how the experts do it, and the experts are the...

Driving Instructors.

Their job is to train people for the most compliance-oriented task in society. They undertake this task in a particular way...

...and it's *not* with rewards and consequences.

Imagine how foolish it would be if, after your first classroom lesson, the instructor said, "All right, students. The cars are outside. Go and try out everything you just learned. If you bring the car back in one piece, you will get half your fee refunded. Anyone who has an accident will have to cover any increase in our insurance rates. That should motivate you to drive carefully. Good luck."

Obviously, no driving school would stay in business long if they operated this way!

Here's How It's Really Done:

After the first lesson about rules of the road, the instructor takes you out to the car and sits right next to you because compliance training requires direct supervision. You can't do it from a distance.

Then the instructor gives you a whole series of directions governing every *small* action. After each one, he (or she) provides some feedback so you know how you're doing. It sounds like this:

"First, put on your seat belt. Right.

Now, start the car. Okay.

Put the car in drive. That's it.

Check your mirrors and look over your shoulder. Good.

Now, pull out slowly. You got it."

If you don't do it right, the instructor stops you and makes you start over. This isn't punishment. It's correction. Take note of what you don't hear in this training routine.

No choices, no bargains, no threats.

The most important strategies for compliance-training are direct supervision and direct instruction. It's also important to start with small compliances because this allows for the constant repetition that creates good habits. Mistakes are corrected and desired actions repeated.

Now let's take a look at what this means for children.

From Driver Training to Child Training

When children are well trained, this is how compliance works for them as well. They follow your instructions because they always follow your instructions - it's a habit. This is the third secret of discipline:

When children are well trained, it's habit-forming.

How do you do this with children?

Remember that compliance is built on little compliances - lots of them. This is the exact opposite of behavior management which teaches you to ignore all the small stuff. (Unless you are very careful, ignoring can cause all sorts of problems.) Parents usually start this training when their children are two years old. Here's a typical example:

Let's say you have a daughter, Andrea. She comes up to you and demands, "I want a drink!"

You say, "Excuse me?"

"May I have a drink?" (That's one compliance.)

"What's the magic word?"

"Please?" (That's two compliances.)

"Yes. Here you are. What do you say?"

"Thank you." (That's three.)

As you do these small compliances, you are building a kind of "momentum" for compliance. A child who has complied with your last 15 directions is very likely to do number 16. The frequency of your directions, along with the lack of choice provided, has prompted the child to respond out of the non-thinking part of the brain, the part where habits are maintained.

This momentum is exactly what you have to develop if you want your child to follow through on chores, school work and other tasks.

Training Games

Certain games and activities are wonderful devices for training compliance. They are designed so that children follow small directions from adults. Because the games are fun, children readily play along, not realizing that they are being taught a very important lesson. Compliance training games include Simon Says, calisthenics, rhythmic clapping, unison reading or singing, and dancing the Macarena.

It's Just Routine

Obviously, you can't do 10 or 15 small compliances before every large compliance. This is where routines come in. As often as possible, you should work a sequence of compliances into a routine.

This saves you a great deal of trouble because routines constantly reinforce all those small compliances which are so important.

Notice that driving instructors use routines to govern your actions when you enter a car. That way, even if your mind is elsewhere, you will always do certain things such as fastening your seatbelt.

Most people rely on routines when they first wake up in the morning because their brain isn't in gear yet. Whenever they get out of routine, there is a real danger that something critical (like shaving or make-up) will be overlooked. Routines are especially useful for bedtime, when it's important to shut off the thinking part of the brain so sleep will come easily (as you will see in the next example).

You Know a Child is Well Trained When...

...you go to visit a friend who is particularly good with discipline. While the two of you talk, her seven-year-old son watches television. She lets him know that he has 15 minutes till bedtime. In a few minutes, she says, "Time for bed, son."

Off goes the television and he starts getting ready. A few minutes later, with teeth brushed and pajamas on, he announces that he's ready. She goes to his bedroom, rubs his back, tucks him in, talks to him about tomorrow and kisses him goodnight. Then she returns to continue the conversation.

You are sitting there in amazement. "How do you do that?" you ask.

"Do what?"

"Get him to go to bed that way."

"I don't know. He always goes to bed that way."

That's right. He always goes to bed that way. It's a habit, supported by routines. Not that it is always this easy. Even this parent will find bedtime difficult at the end of vacation times and maybe even after long weekends (or weekends spent at the other parent's house in the event of a family separation). During such times, routines are often lost and the parents have to work extra hard to get the children back into routine.

Teachers have just as much difficulty explaining good classroom routines and discipline. Go into a classroom where all the students are quietly working. Ask the teacher how he or she is able to get all the students to work so well. Chances are, the teacher will be hard pressed to answer the question. It's always hard to share strategies that you don't consciously develop and think about on a daily basis. The value in the classroom, of course, is that far less time is spent on reacting to misbehavior and far more time on learning.

The Sound of 'Move It'

Listen to the way adults speak to children these days and you will hear those "If...then..." sentences all the time. When discipline gets back on track, you will hear more of this instead:

"No."

"First, pick up your game."

"No fighting!"

By the way, you won't hear the word, "Okay?" on the end of any of these statements. This is a very bad habit that many adults have fallen into lately. They word their commands, "No fighting, okay?" The children are not in charge and you don't need their approval.

Does Compliance Training Worry You?

Many people get a little anxious when they read this chapter. They feel that compliance training sounds very similar to the old days when discipline made children passive and submissive. That's not the case at all and it's very important that parents and teachers recognize the difference.

Remember the three parts of discipline. Back when children were passively submissive to authority, we were over-focussed on training. Little was done in the way of teaching skills and even less on the provision of choices which would allow children to develop independence. Now, we are over-focussed on choices and we overlook the training part of discipline. As happens so often, the pendulum swings from one end to the other. What we need is a balance of all three parts of discipline.

Once again, driving instructors provide an excellent example. They themselves are taught to create certain behaviors as habits and certain behaviors as skills. Good habits include looking in the rear view mirror (approximately every 20 seconds if you are well trained), fastening your seat belt, signalling turns, and looking over your shoulder when you change lanes.

Skills include driving in slippery conditions, parallel parking, and passing other cars safely. These are thinking activities that require the use of driver judgment.

Clearly, driving instructors know exactly what they want to accomplish with the discipline required by drivers. We need to be this clear with children as well. Certain habits are desirable but we don't

want everything to be treated as a habit. We don't want our children to operate like robots. Good habits for children include:
- ▸ obeying instructions which involve safety and health,
- ▸ obeying instructions which involve responsibilities,
- ▸ courtesy and manners,
- ▸ routines such as bedtime and getting ready for school,
- ▸ tidying up after oneself.

Remember that during compliance training, adults must be responsible for ensuring that directions given to children are legitimate and appropriate. It would clearly be irresponsible to train children to do what they are told to do and then instruct them to do something wrong.

Training Camp

Professional sports teams start each season with a training camp. Every day, the players do drills and calisthenics. These activities are designed to make certain responses automatic, because there is no time to think about them during a game. Players also learn to respond to instructions from coaches without arguing. Without training camp, the players would not be ready when the real games begin. During the season, if the team goes into a slump, they aren't punished. Instead, the coach decides that it's time to get back to the "fundamentals". By doing this, the coach re-establishes the routines that have been lost over time.

If training camps are important for highly paid adults who are at the peak of their professional abilities, then they are certainly important for children. Good teachers do this training during the first two weeks of each school year. Then, they renew the routines whenever students return from holidays.

It's simply a matter of good discipline.

There's Nothing Quite Like It

Ironically, although parents and teachers are reluctant to do compliance training with children, they appreciate it in their own lives. When adults have days where everything is a thinking activity and routines are nonexistent, they end up agitated and irritable.

In response, many will go and put themselves in the hands of a compliance trainer, someone who will tell them to do hundreds of little things and they will mindlessly, unthinkingly, comply. So will the other 40 people who are there, probably because their days weren't any better. It's an activity called line dancing.

Now there are 40 people organized into lines. The leader turns on the music and starts to move. All the adults follow right along and make the same moves. Nobody complains. Nobody says, "This isn't fair. It infringes on my personal freedom of choice." Instead, they make comments like, "Isn't this relaxing at the end of a long day?" That is because they don't have to think.

At the end of each day, most of us like to shut off the thinking part of our brain for a little while. It's relaxing. After, we feel refreshed and capable of concentrating on the thinking tasks again. Other activities that we use for this purpose include karate, Tai Chi, running, swimming laps, knitting and even computer games.

Children need this as well. These days, many of them have to think their way through every part of the day. Many parents no longer stress routines and nothing is predictable. Children have to stay alert and deal with constant change in the home environment. In schools, teachers have also decreased the use of routines. No longer do children have to line up quietly, speak in unison, exercise with prescribed moves or do other repetitive activities. It truly is a "think for yourself" world.

Too often, we forget that children struggle to get through days like this the same as we do. They also become agitated, irritable and unproductive. Children need a portion of each day to be governed by routines so they can take some time away from active thinking. They need structure.

Quick Tips

Who's Choice?

Children have to learn which choices are theirs and which choices belong to adults. One way to teach them is to use very specific phrases such as, "parent choice" or "teacher choice". Then, of course, there are the other times when you can honestly say, "It's up to you. The choice is yours".

Chores

Most chores are boring and tedious. If you think about them, you will get frustrated and switch to something else that is more interesting. This is why chores must be treated as non-thinking activities. As you do them, think about something else. Have music playing or turn on the television.

Behavior management would have you treat chores as thinking activities. To accomplish this, you would pay your children their allowance in return for doing their chores. If you do this, it won't be long before the children avoid the chores, hoping they will still get their allowance anyway. If they get part-time jobs, they won't do the chores any more because they will already have enough money.

Chores are important. By doing them, children learn to handle responsibilities. They must also learn to contribute *unconditionally* to the family. This won't happen if you make deals, like paying allowance, to get the chores done. Instead, set up good routines. Then, teach your children to think about other things while they are doing their chores. It's a skill they will use forever.

"No Means No"

When you say "No", it is a signal to your children. You want them to stop doing something and it isn't up for discussion. Essentially, this means, "This is not your choice. Don't even think about it."

Unfortunately, many adults are willing to change their minds. All it takes is for the child to whine, plead, have a temper tantrum or use a guilt trip (Dad lets me do it. I hate you.). Understand what it means when you give in on this. Besides giving the message that you don't mean what you say, you are also allowing your children to get their brains in gear on an issue that was supposed to be a non-thinking response. As a result, they will try to outwit you every time that you deny them something or attempt to stop their misbehavior. You don't want this.

When you say "No", stick with it.

Critical Mass

"Critical mass" is the point at which a chain reaction starts, usually in a bomb. Ironically, it also applies to behavior. Compliance can only be maintained if the majority of people obey rules and directions. Then, for the few that don't, corrections and penalties have a realistic chance of keeping them in line.

However, all it takes is for a few extra individuals to disobey a rule and suddenly, the chain reaction starts. Soon, others begin to join in and, before long, the rule-breakers are in the majority. At this point, it is exceedingly difficult to recover control.

Driving is a good example. If only a few people speed or ignore a particular stop sign, others will continue to comply. If more people join in, however, there is a point at which the misbehavior takes on a life of its own. It isn't long before most people are speeding or ignoring the stop sign.

So when you are dealing with groups of children, don't let misbehavior catch on. Stop it when it first arises. If it reaches the critical mass and the chain reaction starts, watch out. That's when the behavior builds on itself and it will be very difficult to stop.

"Make It So"

Rules are important. They provide protection from many of the dangerous situations that are a part of everyday life. They bring structure and predictability to community living, allowing people to live with a reasonable sense of security. Mere words, however, do not make rules. They exist only when those in a position of authority require compliance. In other words, enforcement is a critical part of this process.

This leads us to the fourth secret of discipline:

Rules worth having, are worth enforcing.

When you undertake the task of establishing rules, you must make a commitment to ensuring that the rules are obeyed. This requires time and energy, but there is no other way to make this part of discipline work.

Whenever the word enforcement is mentioned, people immediately think about punishment. In many ways, the two words have become almost synonymous. This is because discipline, for many years, has relied on consequences and punishments to do this job. When parents and teachers deal with disobedient children, they are always on the lookout for new, easy-to-apply consequences that will make children do what they are told to do. It doesn't take very long to realize that there aren't very many effective consequences.

There are times when parents and teachers may become so desperate to keep control that they threaten to impose huge consequences. For instance, they may ground a child for weeks or even months at a time. Other common threats include never taking a child on a trip again or never returning to a particular restaurant. Clearly, such consequences are unfair. They inevitably evoke a great  deal of anger and resistance from the child, which may elicit an even greater punishment.

This is not the way we want to treat our children and it certainly isn't the kind of problem-solving that we want to model for them. This situation arises when people rely on consequences to do things that consequences are incapable of doing. Although they are sometimes necessary, consequences are only one element of enforcement and they are not the primary response. Here are a few steps which will help you get back on track with enforcement:

Start Small

When behavior management came into vogue, many parents and teachers complained that it was excessively time consuming. One could spend all day just doing rewards and consequences. "Star" charts covered refrigerators. Stickers and points were handed out in vast quantities.

In response to the complaints, experts suggested that parents and teachers overlook small misbehaviors, a technique commonly called "ignoring". What they didn't say was that ignoring is a very risky technique. In reality, the only misbehavior you should ignore is attention-seeking behavior because it is the only behavior which responds to ignoring. But if you ignore defiance, it will escalate. This happens because children believe that:

> ### *Behavior you ignore*
> ### *is behavior you permit.*

The real issue of ignoring is that you shouldn't **punish** every little mistake, but this doesn't mean that you do nothing. Compliance training requires adults to govern the small, almost incidental, actions of children. Driving instructors certainly don't overlook minor infractions. If you don't look over your shoulder when you change lanes, they stop you and insist that you repeat the behavior correctly. (Corrections and "do-overs" are discussed in detail in chapter ten.)

More Powerful than Punishment

Forget what you've heard about being consistent with punishment. In fact, punishment only works if it's a rare event. If you use it too often, children quickly become immune to its impact. Fortunately, there is something far more powerful that you should be using as your primary strategy for enforcement:

Insistence

You must be absolutely determined that children will do what you tell them to do. You must be willing to persist until they follow through. Develop the mindset that, once you give a direction, there is no question but that the children will do as you say. Then be willing to take their hands and lead them to the task while saying, "Yes, you will. Now do it."

Take a good look at people who are in charge. This includes good coaches, people who organize community events and people who run successful business ventures. Then, of course, there are also lots of great parents and teachers. What you will notice about each one of them is that they rarely threaten punishment.

Instead, they have a certain demeanor, a natural authority that comes through in their tone of voice, in their choice of words and in the way they present themselves. It makes no difference whether they are male or female. They take a no-nonsense approach to their jobs, clearly communicating what they expect and accepting nothing less. This is what leadership is all about.

Think once more about driving instructors. When they start giving instructions, it is absolutely clear that there is no choice. The skills for driving safely are not optional and they are not negotiable.

This is what you must do if you wish to be effective. When you give a direction, insist on compliance. Make it absolutely clear that you will not negotiate. It isn't threats of punishment that do this job.

Rather, you must be willing to take the child and say, "Yes, you will. **This** is the job that you are to do. Now, get on with it." Be prepared to stop them from engaging in any other activity.

Remember the keys to making this work. Forget about yelling, threatening and bargaining. Just supervise and direct. Let them see your natural authority in the way you stand and hear it in your voice.

Authority? What Authority?

Where does this authority come from? It comes from knowing your job. It comes from knowing why you are setting limits and why you are training your children to obey them. It comes from knowing the skills and lessons you want your children to learn. It comes from knowing how important it is for children to grow up responsible and co-operative.

When children question your authority, tell them,
"It's my job."

When they challenge your right to make demands, tell them,
"It's my job."

Discipline is not a popularity contest. Don't worry if your children don't like many of the things you do (and they won't). It is respect that you need, not appreciation - respect for your role as a parent or teacher. The appreciation will likely come later, usually after your children have children of their own.

Punishment's Important Role

As more and more people become concerned about the negative impact of today's discipline, particularly the effect of consequences and punishment, they often make the mistake of going to the other extreme, suggesting that punishment is a purely negative strategy that serves no useful purpose. Their contention is that we shouldn't be using it at all. It's unfortunate that the pendulum always seems to swing from one extreme to the other. Either something is all good or all bad. Usually, there is a healthy medium and so it is with punishment.

Before going on, let's be clear why this section is about punishment and not about logical consequences which would be recommended by most experts. The reason is simple. In real life, logical consequences are rare. This is because the logic of a consequence must be in the eye of the receiver, not the giver. Very few children see the logic of a consequence when it is being given. If punishment is how it feels, then punishment is what it is. When children miss out on a school trip or are not allowed to go out with their friends, they have been punished and there is no sense trying to sugar-coat it. Let's call it what it is and communicate to children why it is being used.

Punishment has an important role to play in discipline, but it is not what you think it is. Punishment will not teach children to be responsible and co-operative (as you will see in chapter 10). It will never replace supervision and direction. What punishment does do, however, is give a clear message that:

"No means No!"

Punishment tells children that you mean what you say and children need this message. Punishment may also bring misbehavior to a stop and this is important as well.

If you understand punishment's role, then you will understand that a big punisher is rarely required. Even a short time out, say about two minutes, will give a child a clear message. If you find yourself using bigger and bigger punishers, then you are probably trying to use punishment to do a job that it is not intended to do.

Remember that punishment only works if it's a rare event.

The Big Message

There are times when adults must use a big punishment with children, times when the offense has been so serious that it requires a much clearer statement than any time-out could give. So be it. It would be absolutely foolish to suggest that big punishments should never be used. If students bring weapons to school, for instance, a suspension is clearly appropriate.

When you reach this point, avoid giving the punishment out of anger. Your anger only makes it easier for the child to feel that the punishment is unfair and to ignore the point that you are trying to make. Instead, you should feel a certain sense of sorrow. After all, other ways of working with the child have obviously failed. It is natural to feel sad that the child has gone down this particular road in life.

Throughout the course of a major punishment, keep contact with the child. If, for instance, the punishment is a suspension from school, consider having the child attend for a few minutes each day. These few minutes allow adults to judge the child's state of mind. The time together allows them to stay in touch, which will be very important to the child's progress once the suspension is over.

Similarly in the home situation, avoid sending children to their room and then acting as if they are not in the house. Talk to them. Try to keep them involved in the ordinary functions of the home. Their punishment won't last forever and they have to come out behaving better than when they went in.

Zero Tolerance

Over the past few years, the term "zero tolerance" has become very popular. It has also been widely misunderstood. Contrary to popular belief, zero tolerance is not a punishment issue. It cannot be accomplished by changing rules from, "If you fight, you will go to the Principal's office", to, "If you fight, you will be expelled."

Zero tolerance is an issue of how we communicate expectations. The best example involves the problem of impaired driving. Years ago, everyone knew the penalty for this infraction, the same way they knew the penalty for speeding. The information was discussed openly. "If you drink and drive, you will get a $300.00 fine and lose six demerit points." Unfortunately, once people start drinking, they stop caring about the consequences. Because too many people were dying, lawmakers doubled the fines and instituted jail terms. Nothing changed. Drinkers still didn't care about the penalties.

Then, society moved toward zero tolerance. Instead of bigger fines, millions of little signs went up in car windows all across the nation. Each one said, "Don't drink and drive!" No choices. No discussion of penalties. Just don't! In other words, don't even think about it. Exactly. When we communicate certain actions as being unthinkable, that's zero tolerance.

Respect for Authority

Many parents and teachers worry about using their authority. What if children have no respect and won't do what they are told to do? We have already discussed three of the keys for gaining respect. The first is to build compliance on many small compliances so that children get in the habit of doing what you say.

The second is to present yourself as being in charge. Much of it is in the way you stand and the way you speak. Once again, think about coaches in various sports. Think about driving instructors. Compose yourself the way they do. You have the natural authority that comes from being in a position of great responsibility. Use it and communicate it. Tell children that you are doing what you're supposed to be doing, that you're teaching them to be responsible, co-operative individuals.

Now, here are a few more ways of helping children learn respect for authority:

▸ Respect is a two-way street. If you disregard their rights and needs, it's going to be very difficult for you to teach them to respect the rights and needs of others. This is particularly important during their teen years as they develop independence. Nothing frustrates teenagers as much as adults who have no understanding or respect for adolescent needs.

▸ Model the behaviors that you want to see in the children. If you want them to be courteous, then you should be courteous. Otherwise, children may perceive your rules and directions as arbitrary and unfair. Keep in mind, though, that this doesn't apply to behavior that is considered acceptable for adults, but not for children. For instance, you don't have to go to bed at the same time as your children. Neither do you have to tell the same type of jokes. Children need to learn that adulthood brings certain rights and privileges.

Some parents find it difficult to stop their children from doing activities that the parents do. One of the best examples is smoking. Just because you smoke is no reason to allow your children to become addicted. Don't feel guilty about saying "No". That is what discipline is all about.

Do you remember the camel story from chapter two? Discipline is the way we protect our children and help them learn from the experiences of others. Because you know the dangers of smoking, it's your job to teach your children to choose a better path.

▸ Use your authority wisely. Authority is always open to abuse and you must work hard to avoid falling into the trap. Be very careful not to rely on physical punishment. Neither should you make punishments excessive.

Dear Ann:
Take Two

Now let's return to the trials and tribulations of "Wigged Out". How would these compliance training strategies change the way that she handles the problem with her daughters. Is there an alternative to simply giving up and complaining that "kids will be kids"? Is it possible to get them to clean up their room?

Absolutely. Do you remember the keys for compliance training, the ones that we learned from driving instructors?

Provide direct supervision
Give direct instruction
Start small

"Wigged Out" has to go up to the bedroom with her daughters. This is a compliance task and Mom will never accomplish it while standing in the kitchen.

Then, she has to start with small directions.

"Linda, please pick up this book and put it on the bookshelf. Thanks."

"And Joanie, would you please pick up the doll and put it with the other dolls. Right."

Then comes a pop can, a toy and an article of clothing. Bit by bit, the work picks up speed. The pile of garbage in the corner quickly disappears and the dirty clothes find their way to the laundry hamper.

After giving the first few directions, Mom bends over and starts cleaning the bedroom as well, but not because she made another deal like, "If you do half, I'll do half." No deals. She bends over and starts picking up to model for her children how people in caring families help each other with big jobs.

This is how to get the bedroom cleaned. Allowing these girls to be defiant won't teach them to be responsible and co-operative. They need good training and good teaching. They need discipline.

Creating the Right Environment

Giving small instructions helps lessen the chances of non-compliance. Of equal importance, however, is the thought put into creating the right environment. After all, cleaning a bedroom is a boring task, even at the best of times. It helps if certain things are provided.

Before the task starts, have the girls help make up a tray of drinks and snacks. Take the refreshments up to the room so everyone can have something to eat and drink while they work. Turn on the girls' favorite music or the television if one is available. Finally, remember to set a cut-off time for this type of task. Right up front, tell the girls that you will all work on the bedroom for, let's say, 30 minutes. The rest will be finished later. If you do all these things, the girls will feel that you understand and respect their rights and needs. After all, you are demanding that the bedroom be cleaned out of respect for your rights and needs. You have to model this behavior for them. It's a two-way street.

Many people have a great deal of difficulty with this concept. The reaason is that behavior management has taught them to withhold all the "good stuff" and use it as a bargaining tool.

"If you get your room cleaned, you can have a snack."

"You're not watching any television until your room is clean."

"If you do 30 minutes of hard work, you can have a break."

Most parents and teachers have become accustomed to making deals of this nature. Deals are a very big part of today's discipline. Unfortunately, this means that adults end up withholding the very things that are essential for creating a positive environment (see box on next page).

To get back on track: **make fewer deals,**
provide more supervision,
and give more direction.

Should Children Get What They Deserve?

Today's popular discipline gives children what they deserve. If they do something right, they deserve a reward. If they do something wrong, they deserve to be punished. That will teach them, right?

Wrong! You see, discipline has far more to do with what children need, than with what they deserve. The more we focus on what children deserve, the more they lose out on what they need. In school, for instance, students who misbehave are often denied access to the computer on the basis that they don't deserve it. Working on the computer is seen as a "privilege" which may be used as an incentive.

The problem is that children need to work on the computer to learn the skills required for an increasingly technological world. To use the computer as a privilege is no different than using reading as a privilege. Imagine how absurd it would be for a teacher to say, "If you keep disrupting the class, I won't teach you to read!"

Many students lose out on school trips. But school trips are an essential part of the curriculum. They help children learn that the work done in school can be applied to the real world. No one can say that some children deserve to learn this and others don't.

Parents have to be equally careful. All too often, children lose out on valuable experiences. They may not be allowed to join sports teams or go along on family outings. Often, you will see parents walking away from their children in a store to punish them for not moving quickly enough. This is wrong. Children need security. It has nothing to do with what they deserve.

Part III

TEACH
Skills

Skill Bound

Imagine that your son, Joey, has invited you to visit his classroom and you are sitting at the back watching everyone work. The teacher is working with Joey helping him learn to multiply. After explaining the concept and showing Joey a few examples, the teacher asks Joey to multiply 3 X 4. Joey gives the answer 8 and is immediately sent off to the side of the classroom for a two-minute time out.

When he returns, the teacher tries again and asks Joey to multiply 4 X 5. Joey's answer of 17 results in another time out. The teacher tries one last time. Once again, Joey's answer is wrong and he sits out.

Would Joey learn to multiply?

Of course he wouldn't. If anything, he would learn to hate mathematics. Now, you would never be so foolish as to teach a child this way. **Right?**

Wrong! Thanks to behavior management, you are using this exact technique when you discipline your children. If you don't believe this, just look at how adults usually deal with the all too common problem of rudeness. In school, rude children are often given time outs and detentions. Some have to write lines while others lose privileges. At home, parents respond with scoldings, groundings, time outs and lost privileges.

This is exactly the same technique that you thought was so foolish. If time outs won't teach the skill of multiplication, they won't teach the skill of courtesy.

You already know how to teach skills. After showing Joey how to multiply, you would have him try a question on his own. After he did one correctly, you would have him do several more to lock the skill into his long-term memory. Then, every so often, you would review the skill so he wouldn't forget. The old saying is that "practice makes perfect". People learn skills by doing them correctly over and over. Time outs and other punishments have no place here.

The reason people aren't doing this for courtesy is that behavior management lacks a teaching component. It omits all of the teaching techniques including instruction, practice, correction and review. When it comes to rudeness, for example, the one thing that behavior management never makes children do is the only thing that is truly important. They never have to be courteous.

Instead, behavior management suggests that children can learn responsible behavior simply by experiencing the outcomes of their choices. If this were true, then rude children would learn to be courteous just by experiencing all those time outs, detentions and lost privileges. Typically, however, the only thing they learn is to be immune to all the consequences and punishments and they quickly adopt an "I don't care" attitude.

It's No Different

Responsible behavior must be taught to children in exactly the same manner as mathematics and reading. Once again, think about the way that driving instructors teach their students to parallel park. The student follows the instructor's lead, one step at a time. After accomplishing the task once, the student proceeds to do it several more times.

Coaches teach in exactly the same way. They also use direct instruction to teach students the exact skill which is required. Throughout the practice session, the coach corrects any flaws in the student's technique. Usually, the same skill is practiced for several sessions.

Behavioral skills must be learned the same way. This includes skills such as:

- ▸ courtesy
- ▸ sustained attention
- ▸ getting started on a task
- ▸ returning to task after a distraction
- ▸ conflict prevention and conflict resolution

This leads us directly to the fifth secret of discipline:

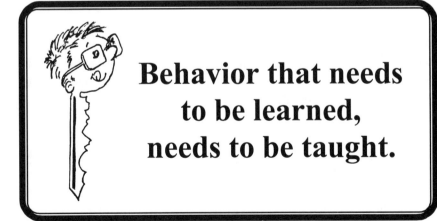

Behavior that needs to be learned, needs to be taught.

"Do-Overs"

If you think in terms of teaching behavior, you will find that the biggest change is in the way you respond to misbehavior. Much of the time, instead of scolding or giving a time out, you should be insisting on a "do-over". Have the child repeat the behavior correctly until he or she gets is right. It sounds simple but very few people do it, thanks to behavior management.

Here are a few examples:

▸ When your children are rude, tell them to start over and speak courteously this time.

▸ When your students run down the school hallway, send them back to walk.

▸ When your children don't look as they cross the road, take them back and have them cross safely.

Here's How it Sounds

Right now, when your children are rude, you probably say something like, "If you talk that way to me again, you will go to your room." Remember that "If...then..." sentences give choices. What this really says is, "If you don't mind going to your room, then being sassy to me is one of the things that you get to do in our home to try to get your own way."

Real discipline wouldn't give this choice. Instead, you would say, "We don't speak that way in our family. Start over." The first sentence sets a limit (the training part of discipline) and the second sentence teaches the child to be courteous through the use of positive practice (the teaching part of discipline).

Caught Speeding!

If you're not convinced that positive practice is more effective than punishment, consider the following scenario.

You're driving to a meeting in another city. Half way through the two hour trip, flashing red lights appear in your rear view mirror and you realize that the police are pulling you over for speeding. You wonder how big the fine will be. "Oh, well," you say to yourself. "There's nothing I can do about it now. Hopefully, this won't take too long and I can still make my meeting."

The officer is now standing at your car door. "You were speeding," he states. "Now, you go all the way back home and do your trip over again at the right speed!" Then the officer attaches a monitoring device to your car to ensure that you do exactly what you've been told to do.

If this happened to you, would you slow down on future trips? You bet you would! Right now, the police are limited to handing out speeding tickets. Many people ignore this potential consequence and go right on speeding. Busy people may even consider the occasional ticket to be the price they have to pay for getting places on time. And, of course, you quickly learn to watch for supervision, just like children do. You slow down when you see a police car and speed up once you're out of sight. Welcome to the world of rewards and consequences.

Most of the time, this is all that you need to do. Skills are learned through positive practice, through multiple repetitions of the correct behavior.

The best way to make this happen is to use the same strategy that was discussed back in Chapter 8. Your most important and most powerful tool for having children practice their skills is your *insistence*. You must convey to the children that they have no choice in this matter, that you are in charge, and that they will do as instructed. Don't let any doubt creep into the conversation.

Remember:

A child who is never required to act appropriately, never will.

But what happens if they refuse?

First, start by repeating your instruction. Make your tone of voice a little more serious this time. If this is met with another refusal, consider taking the child by the hand. Guide the child through the task. Obviously, not every task lends itself to this approach and one wouldn't want to do this with an adolescent. Nonetheless, it is a valuable approach whenever it is appropriate.

If the child refuses yet again, use whatever minor punishment is required to get the message across that you mean what you say. Remember that this is the main value of punishment. Then, bring the child back to do the task correctly. Whatever you do, don't forget this last step. Most parents and teachers have been led to believe that when a punishment is over, discipline is finished.

Finished? It hasn't started yet!

Contrary to what behavior management has taught you, punishment won't create responsible behavior. Only positive practice will do that. When the time-out is over, make sure that the child comes back and speaks courteously. When you think of it, this was the only real issue in the first place.

> *Most of the times when we punish children,*
> *we actually didn't need them punished.*
> *We needed them to behave correctly.*

The Real "Breakfast of Champions"

When children are asked to practice good behavior, they rarely respond positively. Usually, they act as if they are being punished. They can throw up so much resistance that adults may drop their demands. It's just not worth it.

Sometimes, it's all in the presentation.

Ask your child to tell you why Michael Jordan continues to practice handling and shooting the basketball. After all, he is already the best. Why would he keep practicing every day?

Why does Barry Bonds take batting practice?

Why does Tiger Woods work on the driving range and the putting green every day?

These people have already made it to the top of their respective sports. They earn megabucks! If anyone should be able to miss the daily practice sessions, it would certainly be these superstars.

Children should learn to see practice as the only way to develop a skill, and the only way to maintain a skill. Plus, when you are part of a team, everyone participates because individual independence is overridden by team needs. At school, a child's team is the learning community. At home, it's the family.

So tell children that it's time for batting practice. And remember - when players are in a slump, the response isn't punishment. They take *extra* batting practice!

Quick Tips

Use a "Do-Over" Cue

Nothing changes a child's tone of voice quicker than the presence of a few friends. The need to sound independent or "macho" often leads to rudeness and refusals. Most parents are reluctant to correct their children in front of other children for fear of embarrassing them. At the same time, however, it is important that misconduct not be overlooked.

To handle this situation in a way that satisfies everyone, trying using a physical cue or prompt. Almost anything will do as long as your child knows what it means and it is virtually invisible to other children. One example would be to twirl a finger in a circular motion near to your shoulder. This motion would mean, "Start over." Using a cue of this sort, you can discipline your child in public without causing any embarrassment.

It's Okay to Have Fun

Children shouldn't have fun when they are being punished, but practice works better when it is enjoyable. Good teachers understand this principle. They spend a great deal of time designing interesting tasks for students. The obvious reason is that students willingly participate in tasks which are interesting, even when they involve practice. The same is true at home.

If your children have to practice the appropriate behavior for visiting a restaurant, make the activity interesting. Put a tea towel over one arm and pretend that you are a waiter. Make a pretend menu. Laugh. Do likewise for any other practice sessions including how to behave in a supermarket, how to get dressed for school, or how to take a phone message.

"Timing is Everything"

If you try to use positive practice without reading this chapter, you will drive yourself crazy. You will have so many arguments with your children and become so frustrated that it won't be long before you go back to all the old behavior management techniques. The key to positive practice is to know when, and how, to use it. The best way to demonstrate this timing issue is with an example.

Imagine that your son is involved in gymnastics and the coach takes him to a big meet. When the time comes for your son to show what he can do in the vault, the coach starts to talk to him.

"Okay, Jim. You've got a big audience today and all the judges are waiting. Are you ready to do your vault?"

"Yes."

"That's great. Just one thing before you go. Today, I want you to do a whole new vault."

Can you imagine your son's reaction? He would be so stressed out, he would probably have an anxiety attack right then and there.

Obviously, no coach would ever do such a thing to a youngster. Coaches understand that skills have to be prepracticed. In other words, the skills are practiced when they are *not* needed so that the stress level stays down. This prepares the child for the day when the skills must be demonstrated for real. All the practice should make for a great performance.

Teachers have students practice math before the test, so they will do well during the test. Musicians practice when they are not at recitals so they will do well when they are at recitals. And, of course, no one would want an airplane pilot to wait for a crisis before practicng the skills required to deal with the crisis.

Sounds pretty obvious, doesn't it?

Not if you've been using today's popular discipline. Because it's all about learning from experience, it has you teaching bedtime routines *at bedtime!* This is the worst possible time. If you try to do it then, your stress level will skyrocket, as will your child's. Before long, the two of you will be arguing and bedtime will have become an unpleasant experience.

It's not just bedtime that is affected in this way. Today's discipline also has you teaching supermarket skills while you are shopping for groceries, restaurant skills while you are eating in a restaurant, and courtesy skills in the middle of an argument. In schools, teachers often try to teach transition routines during transitions, assembly behaviors during assemblies, and recess behaviors at recess. The obvious result is that people end up very upset.

Behavioral skills are no different than all the other skills. They are best taught when they are *not* needed so the behavior is there when it is needed. This means that bedtime routines are best taught at two o'clock in the afternoon, reviewed at five and again at seven so they will be well learned at nine o'clock when it's really bedtime.

Supermarket skills should be taught when you are not shopping for anything. Start at home if you like. Then, go to the supermarket for a "pretend" shopping. Just pick up a few dry goods. This way, if you have to remove your child from the store, you can leave the cart behind. Nothing will spoil. And, of course, you won't be annoyed because you didn't need any of those items anyway. If everything goes well, then you can do the wonderful educational activity of turning around and having your child figure out where things go back on the shelves. This activity uses many of the early learning skills for reading, grouping and shape recognition.

The value of practicing behaviors when they are not needed is so great that it forms the sixth secret of discipline:

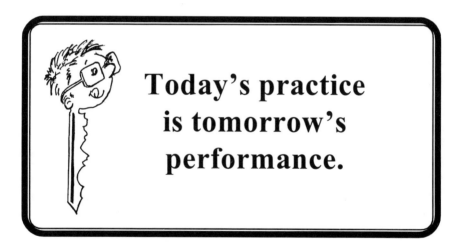

Today's practice is tomorrow's performance.

If you want a great example of this, take a look at school secretaries. They need students to cover the phones at lunch time, so they teach the students how to answer the phone, what to say, how to say it, the exact tone of voice to use, how to take a message, where to put the message and how to get a teacher on the intercom. They teach all these skills when the phone is not ringing, so the students will do well when it does ring. Imagine what it would be like if the students were allowed to learn from experience. They would sit around until the phone finally rang. The first student would pick it up and

say, "Township School. What do you want?" The secretary would have an anxiety attack of her own and begin yelling, "No. You can't talk to the parents that way!" It's too stressful and everyone gets upset.

Reminders are Better than Threats

There is one more lesson that we can learn from coaches. When a child is finally in a real situation and is called upon to demonstrate a particular skill, the coach doesn't do much talking. Instead, the coach simply reminds the child of the key points that were emphasized during training. Think back to our example of the coach taking your son to the gymnastics meet. If your son is well trained, this is how the coach will talk to him just before his vault:

"It's your turn, Joey," says the coach. "Do you remember the three things that I taught you about the vault?"

"Yes. Six steps to the take-off, push off of the vaulting horse, and keep my feet together for the landing."

"You got it. Good luck."

That's all. As Joey approaches the test situation, the coach simply reminds him of the key points that were learned during the practice sessions. This is the way that parents and teachers should handle situations as well.

For example, when you are taking your child to the supermarket, you say:

> "Do you remember the three things I taught you about behaving in the supermarket?"

> "Yes. No running, no grabbing, no whining." (You could also use positive wording if you prefer such as "Walk beside you, ...")

> "Right."

If your child isn't old enough to repeat these items, then you say them. Your child merely agrees.

Post-It

No matter how much preparation you do, your children will still make mistakes when they are actually in "test" situations such as the supermarket. When this happens, remember to limit your response to a correction. Say "No" to stop them and then tell them what they are to do. Insist they do it. If necessary, take them by their hands, but resist the temptation to threaten consequences or offer bribes. Also, avoid lecturing them on supermarket behavior. It's neither the time nor the place.

Instead, make a note to remind yourself that more practice is required before the next trip to the supermarket. Put the note up on the kitchen cupboard so it won't be forgotten. When you have some time, have your children rehearse the supermarket skills that need improvement. This practice can occur at any time that is convenient to you.

Although rewards and consequences need to be immediate, learning goes on forever. After all, teachers take years to teach the skills of division and they even take breaks for summer vacations. They simply write notes for the new teachers that will take over when school begins in September.

12 Absence Makes the Worry Grow Stronger

There is an old saying, "Out of sight is out of mind." This may be good when it comes to chores that we wish to avoid. That is not the case, however, when it's our children who are out of sight. Most of us worry. We know the mischief that children get into when they are not supervised.

As you reflect on everything that you've learned so far about today's discipline, this shouldn't come as any surprise. Remember the value system that today's discipline develops in our children. It teaches them to do what is advantageous, not what is right. Hence, it is only natural for them to "take advantage" of situations.

Children who have this value system look forward to situations where they are left unsupervised because they have the opportunity to do whatever they feel like doing.

That is what makes this chapter so important. As you teach your children the skills for being responsible and co-operative, there is one skill that you won't want to miss. From the time when your children are very young, teach them to use self-discipline. If you do, they will learn to make good decisions, even when you are not there to supervise.

Revelation

To be able to teach this skill, you must be able to see it, and hear it, in action. I still remember the day this happened to me and it changed the way I discipline children. Let me share this experience with you.

I was visiting a grade 2/3 class when the teacher explained to her students that she would be leaving the classroom for a few minutes. They were to continue working quietly. She then asked them a fascinating question. "What does this mean you need?"

Up went the hands and one child answered, "Self-discipline." Having never heard this word come out of a child's mouth before, I was naturally amazed, but it didn't stop there. The teacher continued, "What does self-discipline mean?"

Up went the hands again and another child answered, "It means we behave when you're not with us, exactly the same way we behave when you are standing right next to us." I thought about this answer for a minute and realized that, for young children, that is precisely the meaning of self-discipline. The teacher and I both left the room but I stopped in the hallway to watch the students from a distance. Nothing happened. The students continued to work as if their teacher was still with them in the classroom.

Later, I asked the teacher how she accomplished this extraordinary feat. She explained that her students practiced this skill from the very first day of school. By standing right beside students, she would prompt them to show their best behavior. Then, she challenged them to maintain this behavior as she moved farther and farther away. First, it was one step, then two. Before long, the teacher could be at one end of the room and the students at the other end would still behave well, just like she was standing right next to them. Within a few more weeks, they had learned how to maintain their behavior when the teacher left the room, first for a few seconds and then for longer periods of time.

Listen to the Difference

Now, here comes the most important part. When students had problems, this teacher would speak to them in a very different manner. These days, when adults are dealing with kids' disputes, they normally ask , "What happened?" The next question is, "Why did you do that?" This "why" question is designed to elicit the information that adults need to decide who was right and who was wrong. The one who was right would be praised and the one who was wrong would be punished. That's behavior management.

This teacher used very different words. When her students had problems, she still asked "What happened?" Then, she said,

"Would you have made the same decision if I had been standing right next to you?"

Now, there is an interesting question. Usually, students would say, "No." The next question was obvious:

"Why do you need me standing next to you for you to make a good decision?"

Think about this for a minute. These questions go right to the heart of discipline. As children mature, they should be able to make good decisions without adult supervision. This is what real independence is all about.

The Search for Independence

As children grow older, they naturally look forward to the time when parents and teachers won't be "looking over their shoulders". They view independence as a time when they can "do their own thing". Unfortunately, today's discipline has influenced our thinking so much that many parents and teachers now tend to agree with this view. This is not what our children need to learn.

By the time they start to become independent, children must have a more balanced view of independence. Real discipline teaches children that personal rights are balanced with responsibility and that the rights and needs of others must be taken into account. It also teaches them to see every unsupervised situation as an opportunity to demonstrate responsibility, which brings us directly to the seventh secret of discipline:

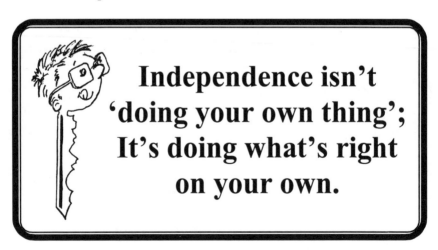

Independence isn't 'doing your own thing'; It's doing what's right on your own.

If you want to decrease your worry lines, this is what you must teach your children. First, you use your presence to ensure that they do what is right. Then, teach them to do it on their own. Here are a few examples of what it should look like, both at home and at school:

At home, children who have mastered this skill behave well:
- when their parents leave them in charge of the house
- when friends come over to play
- when they go out into the community

At school, students who have mastered this skill behave well:
- for occasional teachers
- when the teacher is working with other students
- when they are working alone in a room

Start Young

Start when your children are young. At home, this means during the toddler years. At school, start in Kindergarten. Obviously, toddlers don't have the language to carry on the conversation that was previously described. That's okay. Start with the important lesson that "No means no," even when you are not in the room. For instance, once you have taught them not to touch certain items, make sure they understand that it also applies when you leave. Then, insist that they play properly and speak politely whether you are in the room or not. When your children are old enough to understand, start using the self-discipline statements in your daily communication. Ask the question, "Would you have done that if I were here with you?"

Although you should start teaching this skill when children are young, this doesn't mean that you stop when they get older. Imagine that you have a teenage son, James. He earns his driver's licence when he is 16 and enjoys his new-found freedom. To be sure he is safe, you require him to keep you informed about where he goes and when he will return. These rules work well until his 18th birthday. Suddenly, the phone calls come to an end.

When you demand an explanation, your son replies, "I'm 18 now. I shouldn't have to call home." Recognize that this answer would be supported by today's learn-from-your-own-experience discipline, but real discipline is different. If you want to do real discipline, here is the rest of the conversation:

"I realize that you are 18 now, but that doesn't mean you don't call home. You still call but it's for a different reason. Before, you did it because I told you to. Now that you're 18, you do it on your own because you understand that I worry."

That's real independence.

Important?

If you don't think this skill is important, imagine that your son (or daughter) has turned 17 and is out driving a car alone for the first time. You want him to drive without you in the car, the same way he drove when you were sitting in the passenger seat....so he will live! That's how important this skill is. If you don't teach it, your son will take advantage of being alone in the car, put the "pedal to the metal" and possibly end up in a serious accident.

So understand that this is an important skill that you must teach your children from when they are very young. They should constantly here those words, "Why do you need me with you for you to make a good choice?"

Part IV

MANAGE Choices

Decisions, Decisions

As children grow up, they need to make more and more choices on their own so they will learn how to handle the demands that await them in adulthood. But how do you know when it's the right time to give them more freedom? How do you know when they are ready?

The best answer to this question came from a colleague of mine who is the mother of two children. One day, she was dealing with her son and he replied with a rather terse, "I don't care!" Mom's response tells you much of what you need to know about your role as a parent or teacher. It will also dramatically affect the way you explain decisions to your children.

**After her son said, "I don't care,"
Mom replied,**

**"That's okay, son, because I do
and that's why this is my choice.
Someday, when you care about it
as much as I do,
it will become your choice."**

Exactly! When children are very young, they are both impulsive and shortsighted. They do whatever they feel like doing without any consideration for the risks. They don't comprehend the dangers involved in their decisions. Adults do. We know what happens when children run out on the road, when they play with matches, or when they get into a stranger's car. We understand the importance of going to school and the impact of dropping out.

This is why real discipline empowers parents and teachers to make decisions for children until children are mature enough to make the decisions for themselves. The eighth secret of discipline makes this very clear.

Keep responsible decisions in responsible hands.

This is what raising children and teaching children is all about. Unfortunately, you've been taught behavior management. You've been taught that children should be allowed to make their own choices and they will learn responsibility by experiencing the outcomes of their choices. Well, the more you've bought into this philosophy, the more confused your children will be. They won't know which choices genuinely belong to them and which ones belong to adults. Let's take a look.

Chores

One of our jobs is to teach children how to handle the chores and responsibilities that are part of family life. We must also ensure that children contribute in a meaningful way to their families and to their communities. When children are young, they don't understand the importance of chores and responsibilities. This means that these jobs are adult decisions until such time as children are old enough and mature enough to undertake them for themselves.

When children clean their bedrooms, they learn organizational skills and the proper care of possessions. Food preparation provides children with training in a valuable life skill. The careful washing of dishes and countertops teaches the importance of cleanliness for good health. As adults, it's our job to teach our children these skills and to ensure that the children do their part in the home. This is the reason why the jobs are assigned. It has nothing to do with allowance. Give them an allowance so they learn how to handle money, but give them chores and responsibilities so they learn how to be responsible.

Grades and Marks

This section isn't just for teachers. How well children do in school is everyone's concern. Today's discipline has had an extraordinary impact on the evaluation of school work. Most parents and teachers now accept the notion that students who hand in work that is incomplete and disorganized should receive a low or failing grade. The assumption is that the students will reflect on their poor performance and decide to do better work in the future.

Unfortunately, this philosophy only works for the students who care about grades and are motivated to do well. What about the students who don't care? What about the students who don't understand the long-term impact of a poor education?

Who Sets the Standards?

From Mrs. Smith's point of view, the problem was perplexing. In the interests of encouraging her Grade 6 students to develop self-motivation and effective decision-making, she had designed an assignment in which the students could select their final grade in advance. They would then sign a contract stipulating the work required to fulfil the requirements for that grade. As long as the student completed the work in accordance, then the selected grade would be received. In this way, the students would gain greater control over their grades and should be motivated to establish high personal expectations.

Unfortunately, one student's decision created a considerable flurry of consternation. Jim contracted for a "C", and proceeded to do the work required to fulfil the criteria in the contract. His parents, however, were deeply concerned because Jim had always been an "A" student. A discussion with the teacher provided little satisfaction, nor did a subsequent meeting with the principal. On both occasions, they were reminded that Jim was the one who had made the decision to receive a low mark and they should be communicating their displeasure to him.

The parents, however, had a very different point of view. They believed that it is a fundamental part of every teacher's job to ensure that students work up to their potential. Jim's decision, they maintained, was not his to make! As an "A" student, he should have been expected to submit "A" quality work. What do you think?

When faced with the possibility of receiving low grades, their typical response is, "So, give me an F. I don't care. Marks don't really count." The only thing that these students learn from low marks is to turn off and tune out when it comes to school.

When children don't care, adults have to. It's the job of teachers and parents to set standards for children until the children care about the standards for themselves. Listen to the difference. Joey turns in work which is incomplete and disorganized. With today's discipline, the teacher would say, "Joey, if you hand in your work this way, it will get an F. Maybe you should take it back and fix it up. If you do, then you will get a passing grade." This is just like saying, "If you don't mind low marks, you may disregard my instructions and refuse to complete your work." Given this choice, it's very unlikely that Joey would go anywhere near the work, much less complete it. When report card time comes, the parents will undoubtedly be told that Joey's failing grades reflect his own poor choices.

But were they his choices to begin with? Not with real discipline. Since Joey doesn't care about the quality and completeness of his work, the teacher makes the decisions. When Joey hands in the work, the teacher says, "Joey, your work is disorganized and incomplete. I'm not accepting it. Take it back. Fix it up. I'm not marking it until it's done." Marks were never intended to be hijacked by behavioral experts for use as rewards and consequences. They are evaluation tools designed to provide feedback about a student's understanding of concepts, depth of insight and use of analytical skills. This is one area where we truly need to get "back to the basics".

Courtesy

Children always seem to think that courtesy is optional. Now, many adults see it the same way - nice when it happens, but not particularly important in the overall scheme of things. Others actually believe that courtesy is a relic, something that was popular in the past but which is hardly necessary in the modern world. In any case, it's so hard to get children to be courteous these days that many adults simply stop trying.

It's truly unfortunate that something so important has been downgraded. Courtesy is far more than a pleasant "extra". It forms the foundation for co-operative interactions between people. Courteous words and actions speak volumes. They communicate a willingness to take another person's rights and needs into account. This means that courtesy is not only part of co-operation, but it is a significant part of responsibility as well. Far from being an optional "extra", courtesy is one of the basic skills which adults must teach to children. It's an adult choice until such time as children understand the importance that courtesy plays in our daily interactions and decide to be courteous on their own.

Dealing With the Ups and Downs of Childhood

Life's road is anything but smooth. There are lots of potholes, especially throughout the teenage years. Our children suffer through hormonal changes, emotional ups and downs, break-ups and peer pressure. When they are dealing with the latest crisis, the one thing you can count on is that they don't care about ordinary, everyday issues like chores, homework and marks. That's when you have to take back some of the decisions that you have already turned over to them. You take them back just for a while until they are capable of handling them again. It's not to be mean or to treat them like they are little kids. It's simply that it's your job to care when they don't.

Homes and schools are not democracies.
Adults must be willing to make the decisions
that are adult decisions to make.

The Ties that Bind

Have you ever noticed that many discipline strategies seem to work much better for some people than for others? Well, it's true. That's because the success of various strategies depends upon a variety of factors such as consistency, timing, and the temperament of the child being disciplined. There is one other factor which stands out above all the rest and it can be expressed in a single word:

Whether you are a parent or a teacher, your relationship with a child is the single greatest factor in determining the outcome of discipline. That's because it affects how the child "sees" discipline and, hence, how he or she will respond.

Negative relationships cause children to see discipline as arbitrary and overly restrictive. They feel that adults make unreasonable rules and demands, and that adults don't understand. As a result, these children throw up a wall of resistance in an effort to stop adults from exerting what is they believe is excessive control.

Positive relationships, on the other hand, help children understand that discipline is intended to be beneficial. Children come to realize that rules are imposed in an attempt to maintain safety and security, rather than to keep control. When caring adults become angry and unreasonable, children are usually able to see through the harsh words. They understand that the anger is temporary and that the adult will probably regret the loss of control later. (Apologies all around.)

A positive relationship is so important that it is the basis for the ninth secret of discipline:

Discipline comes best from the heart, Not the hand.

Discipline "from the heart" has the maximum impact on a child because it uses the most natural, and most powerful, rewards and consequences. Young children, in particular, want to please their parents and teachers. They want to be noticed and appreciated.

At the same time, they will exert a surprising amount of self-control in order to avoid displeasing those who care about them. No punishment hurts more or has more impact than the heartfelt disappointment of someone who loves you. Most children would much prefer to spend time in isolation or lose a few privileges. Very few words have to be said to convey this message.

To establish this kind of relationship with a child takes time and attention, understanding and affection. If you have managed to create this bond, protect it by using positive discipline strategies. Here are six special ones to help you along.

Focus on the Positive

How would you feel if your best friend constantly told your other friends about all the things you have done wrong? Then all your friends start to berate you for your mistakes, reminding you over and over that you should be doing better. Before long, you would probably be looking for some new friends. After all, people who really cared about you wouldn't treat you this way. Instead, they would focus on what you do right and show a genuine sense of understanding for your mistakes.

Children are no different. They want the same consideration from the caring adults in their lives. Unfortunately, today's discipline has prompted many adults to overfocus on children's mistakes to the point where misbehavior is the main topic of conversation. Parents complain to each other about their child's actions and relate the stories to relatives. Many teachers maintain 'communication books' for difficult students. The books are sent home regularly, informing parents of everything a child has done wrong.

This constant negative communication damages the relationships between adults and children, the same as it would between you and your friends. Unless the child's actions are unusually serious, simply deal with the behavior and keep it to yourself. Remember the old saying that, "If you can't say anything nice about someone, don't say anything at all." It still holds true.

"Wipe the Slate Clean"

Here is another time-honoured saying which still holds a great deal of meaning. Nobody likes to be reminded of past transgressions. They're history and nothing can change them. What's really important is how one does today and in the future.

Many children feel that they can never escape their mistakes of the past. Everyone keeps reminding them. This is especially true when parents and teachers set up the "communication books" noted in the previous section. Can you imagine how it would feel to carry home a book that lists everything you did wrong since last September? No wonder children tend to lose these books on the way home. So would you.

Life is hard enough without carrying around past baggage. Help children learn to start each day fresh. Wipe the slate clean. Rather than discuss what they did wrong yesterday, talk about how today will unfold. Help them plan for success.

Don't Back Away from Discipline

I once asked a 12-year-old boy to tell me how his step-mother felt about him. He replied confidently that she loved him. When I asked how he could be so certain, he stated, "Because she makes me do what I'm supposed to do."

Discipline isn't one of the things that children appreciate. They don't want to obey rules and limits. They don't want to practice appropriate behavior. Nonetheless, children understand that it is what parenting and teaching are all about. All those hours spent training, rehearsing, talking and negotiating do not go unnoticed. Children interpret the investment as a sign of caring.

Some parents avoid making demands on their children. They are afraid that their children won't like them. When children know that their parents feel this way, they tend to use it as a weapon to try to get their own way. "You don't love me. Nobody else's parents make them do this. I hate you." And if you are separated, you will hear, "I want to go and live with Daddy (or Mommy)."

Don't worry when your children make comments such as these. Discipline is not a popularity contest. It isn't something that we do so our children will love us. It's what we do because we love them. In any case, it isn't really you that they hate. It's the restrictions that you are placing on them.

Deep down, children know what it means when you invest countless hours on discipline. They know that you would only do this if you loved them. The only time that children are uncertain is when parents and teachers back off of rules and limits. This leaves children uncertain, anxious and insecure. So, never give up.

"Gift" Your Child

Children go through tough times, the same as adults do. When they are struggling, school work and chores tend to be low priorities and are often left unfinished. Rather than overlook the unfinished work, consider doing it for them.

Think about it from the child's point of view. It's a big lift to realize that your teacher has completed your unfinished mathematics for you. It's a great start to the day to find a note on the breakfast table that reads, "The garbage has already been put out by the curb. Have a nice day."

Everyone needs a boost sometimes.
So, give it a try but remember....
No deals.
No reminders that it was really the child's job.
It's a gift.

Lead the Way

Our children learn far more from watching us than from listening to us. It's important that we show them the kind of behavior and attitudes that we want them to show others. When you have a positive relationship with a child, you are modelling a caring attitude along with respect for the rights and needs of others. Your discipline techniques should be just as positive. Be as courteous as possible when disciplining your child. Be willing to listen to the child's point of view. Give credit where credit is due.

Above all, avoid the use of humiliation as a disciplinary tactic. Your immediate response to this suggestion is probably that you would never do such a thing. Unfortunately, it is far more common than we would like to think. Just look at how frequently children are scolded in front of their friends or classmates. As another example, many parents struggle to get their children ready for school in the morning. Some parents solve the problem by dropping the child off at school still dressed in pyjamas. They argue that the strategy is effective because the misbehavior is rarely repeated. That's true. Humiliation is a very powerful strategy. It's also wrong. Positive practice would take a little more time but would work equally well. The only way that children will learn to treat others with respect is if we treat them with respect.

Remember the "do-over" cue (see chapter 10) that can be used when you need to correct children in front of their friends. By using such strategies, you can avoid causing embarrassment which would undermine both your discipline and your relationship. Take note that this is also why you should insist that your children comply with certain dress codes, including hair styles and body piercing. If you go out of your way not to embarrass them in front of their friends, then they shouldn't embarrass you in front of yours. It's a two-way street. This isn't an issue of personal rights and freedoms. It's an issue of respect for the feelings of others. If you don't insist on this, then they will never learn to take the needs of others into account.

Reject Behavior, Not Children

Nothing hurts a child more than rejection. Unfortunately, some of our most common discipline techniques can leave children feeling unwanted. When children are forced to leave a room, the children often feel rejected. They feel that their parents or teachers don't want them. It's important that you don't leave this impression. Be clear with children that it is their behavior that is undesirable, not them. Help them understand that they are welcome when they can behave appropriately. Avoid using statements like, "You're bad." There is a world of difference between bad behavior and bad children.

Set Standards

In an effort to keep children happy and successful, parents and teachers have backed away from setting standards. Instead, there is a tendency to accept whatever work and behavior a child produces. This tolerance for mediocrity acts like an enormous brake on growth. Many children continue to display immature and unproductive behaviors right into their adolescent years.

Standards are essential if children are to recognize success and be affirmed in their efforts. In addition, we must come to the realization that the setting of standards has a significant impact on our relationships with children. Our willingness to set legitimate standards, along with our determination that children will rise to those standards, conveys an unmistakable message that we believe in our children and have confidence in their abilities. In effect, we are saying to children, "We believe that you are bright enough and capable enough to be able to learn this." Now, that is a message that says we care.

Self-Esteem or Self-Indulgence?

Watch out! "Centre of the Universe Syndrome" is making a comeback. Once again, many of our children are developing the attitude that the world should revolve around their personal rights and needs. It happened before when discipline went through its permissiveness stage. We gave and gave to our children and asked for nothing back. As a result, we ended up with a generation of spoiled brats. Now, thanks to today's discipline, it's happening again.

The problem keeps growing as children learn to defeat the rewards and consequences system. Parents and teachers respond by offering bigger deals and threatening bigger consequences, desperately trying to convince children that compliance is worthwhile. The children, as you would expect, are more than happy to watch adults struggle.

For years, behavioral experts have defended these practices. In so doing, they altered our beliefs about some of the most fundamental aspects of child development, particularly the issue of motivation. Other areas of significant change include our use of praise and our concept of self-esteem. Let's take a closer look.

Motivation

Today's discipline is based on the theory that children must be motivated to behave in certain ways. Hence the use of rewards and consequences. Experts contend that adults cannot expect children to do schoolwork, chores and responsibilities unless they somehow motivate the children. Some experts go so far as to suggest that you can't make any child do what they do not wish to do.

Nonsense!

Making children do what they don't want to do
is one of discipline's most important roles.

Children don't want to obey rules. They don't want to wait for meals. Dessert time should be anytime. Homework should be banned, as should bedtimes. This is the way they think. The reason we discipline our children is so they learn to inhibit their desires and comply with external authority.

Look at this in terms of your own life for a moment. Let's use the driving example once again. Suppose you are driving to an important meeting and you are running late. Just before you get to an intersection, the traffic lights turn red. What would you really like to do? You undoubtedly wish you could go through the red light and get to the meeting as soon as possible. Nonetheless, you stop.

This is what your training has done for you. You learned to obey rules regardless of your personal desires. This is the purpose of real discipline.

The danger in today's discipline, with its distorted view of motivation, is that children develop an attitude, and it's not a positive attitude. Children come to believe that they should only be required to do things that are interesting to them. If work is boring, the teacher should make it exciting. If chores are boring, they should be paid for doing them. When they are asked to do jobs, they reply with, "Why should I? What's in it for me? I don't feel like it." Every parent and teacher has heard these comments.

Motivation is Great, But...

Real discipline doesn't rely on motivation. Instead, children are taught the skills for doing tasks that interest them along with the skills for doing tasks that don't interest them. We all know that the world is full of both types of jobs. When adolescents apply for part-time work, they quickly find out that such jobs usually include cleaning washrooms and floors. Adults don't do children any favours by teaching them to only do tasks that are interesting.

To the extent that you are capable of designing tasks to be interesting, go for it. Children rarely balk at doing such activities and this will dramatically reduce the number of confrontations that you have with them. Resist the temptation to use money, however, since it leads to so many other problems. Instead, add in challenges like beating the clock or having a race against someone else. You can even add in a special treat, but not until you readthe part of this chapter that tells you the difference between incentives and bribes.

Then, remember to teach children how to complete boring tasks. This is an important skill. Pauline Thornton, a behavior specialist, refers to this as "perseverance training". For her students, she defines it as "forcing yourself to do something even when you don't feel like it". She teaches the skill to students and then challenges them to persevere on tasks that are deliberately designed to be tedious. If this sounds unusual, that's because it is. Maybe it shouldn't be.

Rewards

Throughout this book, much has been said about the multitude of problems created by the misuse of rewards. The word "misuse" is critical. Rewards have their place and they can be very useful. They are certainly important when it comes to the third part of discipline, the management of choices. Keep in mind, however, that rewards (and consequences) are best used to support the good training and teaching of children, not to replace these elements. Rewards, used correctly, can be very positive and productive. After all, everyone needs a little recognition at times or a little extra incentive.

Remember that, for young children, your relationship is the most powerful reward (just as your disappointment is the most potent consequence). Make time for your children. Show interest in their activities and discoveries. At all times, be genuine.

When you use tangible rewards such as stickers or treats, consider using them in a special way. Think about the power of *"shared rewards"*. Instead of giving a child a sticker, give him (or her) three stickers. He keeps one and gives the others away to friends, classmates, or siblings. It works the same way for cookies, certificates, or the right to play a special game.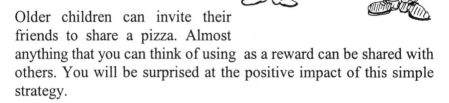

Older children can invite their friends to share a pizza. Almost anything that you can think of using as a reward can be shared with others. You will be surprised at the positive impact of this simple strategy.

When rewards are shared, you don't have to worry about other children being jealous. They won't be tempted to sabotage the child who is working towards a reward because they would be hurting themselves at the same time. Instead, they tend to make supportive comments such as, "Come on, Jason. You can do it." Shared rewards also help in establishing friendships. When one child receives a treat from another child, they will very likely end up playing together.

Incentives vs. Bribes

If incentives are okay and bribes are not, how can you tell the difference? Here is a quick, easy method. Let's say you are prepared to give your daughter $10.00 for cutting the grass. If she can get out of doing the job simply by declining the money, then you were offering a bribe. If she still has to do the job, then it was an incentive.

Listen to the difference. With the bribe, the conversation sounds like this:
"Cut the grass and I'll give you $10.00."
"No, thanks. I don't need the money."
"Okay. I'll cut it but it's your loss."

Now, listen to the conversation that goes with an incentive:
"I need you to cut the grass. I'll give you $10.00 for it."
"No, thanks. I don't need the money."
"That's fine. Now, go and cut the grass."

(Try it. You'll like it.)

Praise

Praise is the most common reward used by parents and teachers. In our efforts to convince children to complete schoolwork and chores, we have fallen into the bad habit of using praise indiscriminately, spreading it on thick just like jam on toast. We do this in the hope that children will respond with increased effort and positive attitudes.

No More Effort Than Necessary

Alexander had just figured out how to put together his 8-piece jigsaw puzzles. For a two-year-old, this was a triumph and he clapped his hands with glee. All four adults who were watching happily joined in the celebration.

Alexander quickly set himself a new challenge. He turned over all three of his puzzles, stating that he could do them all at once. Quickly, eight pieces came together for the first puzzle and he jumped in the air with excitement. The adults clapped and cheered.

On he went to the next puzzle. The first six pieces went together so quickly that Alexander couldn't contain himself. He jumped up and clapped and cheered. Everyone else cheered as well, adding their encouragement. "Keep going. Two more pieces and you'll be finished." But a look of complete disinterest crossed Alexander's face and he turned away from the second puzzle.

On to the third puzzle he went! This time, only four pieces went together before Alexander leaped into the air. Fortunately, the adults had no intention of being outsmarted this time. There was no celebration. Instead, one could hear the clear statement, "No way! Finish it and then we'll cheer." He did. But he never went back and finished the second puzzle.

If you give praise for an unfinished job, then an unfinished job is all you will get. If a two-year-old can figure this out, then you had better believe that every school-age child understands the concept intuitively.

In reality, overly abundant praise usually reduces motivation and creates dependency. (See box on previous page.) Children mature faster and have healthier attitudes when adults reserve their praise for work and behavior which is worthy of recognition. Research suggests that effective teachers have a unique ability to present students with work which is just slightly above what the students believe they are capable of accomplishing. In this way, the students always feel challenged. They strive to reach standards that are held just out of reach.

Self-Esteem

Some of those searching for a solution to the crisis in discipline would have parents and teachers believe that low self-esteem is at the root of many of today's behavior problems. They note that children who are successful and responsible tend to have high self-esteem. However, children who do poorly in school and get into trouble in the community tend to have low self-esteem. On this basis, they argue that raising self-esteem would promote responsible behavior. This theory has been the basis for hundreds of books and videos. Entire programs for raising self-esteem have been produced for teachers to use in their classrooms.

At this point, it is worth remembering the corollary to Murphy's Law which warns that for every complex problem, there is a simple, easy-to-understand wrong answer. Although responsible and successful students may indeed have high self-esteem, this does not mean that raising the self-esteem of difficult students would somehow encourage them to be more responsible and successful. Logic cannot be reversed. Just because all cats are mammals doesn't mean that all mammals are cats. It doesn't work.

In the real world, the most likely result of attempting to raise self-esteem directly is that children will feel much better about themselves while they continue to misbehave.

This is a very real danger. The methods that many people use to raise self-esteem are far more likely to make children self-indulgent. Commonly used strategies include success-only education, where all programs are designed to avoid failure. (In reality, there can be no genuine success without the very real possibility of failure.) Parents and teachers may avoid putting pressure on children or demanding high-quality work. Children may be permitted to express themselves freely without fear of rebuke.

Removed from the criticism which normally follows serious misconduct, children may gradually lose their sense of shame and stop exerting self-control over their actions. They start to rationalize their misdeeds with explanations such as, "I just felt like it. That's all. It made me feel good." To avoid going down this road, remember the tenth secret of discipline:

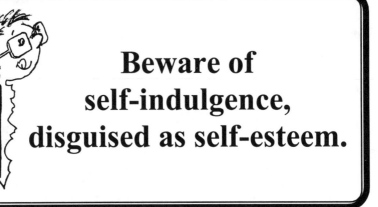

**Beware of
self-indulgence,
disguised as self-esteem.**

Parents and teachers must ensure that the self-esteem of children is firmly rooted in reality. It must be built on a foundation of genuine competence, both academically and socially as well as the ability to personally resolve problems and overcome obstacles. True self-esteem also reflects the development of positive relationships and a sense that one is a contributing member of the community.

There is no evidence to support the effectiveness of separate self-esteem progams for children. The development of positive self-esteem requires much more than the simple act of filling in the blanks on an activity sheet filled with slogans. Neither is it enhanced by having children sitting in groups, extolling their personal virtues to disinterested peers.

If we teach children their academic and social skills along with responsibility and diligence, then they will be well on the road to developing a genuine sense of accomplishment. If we raise our expectations and challenge children to grow to their full potential, then they will experience a lasting feeling of pride. If, along with these skills, we teach them to maintain a balanced view of themselves in relation to the world around them, then they may experience the sense of quiet confidence which is the real trademark of high self-esteem.

16 *A Spoonful of Planning Helps the Conflicts Go Down*

oday's discipline is based on the premise that children should learn from experience. They make their own choices. Adults are supposed to react to those choices. That word "react" is very important. Many parents and teachers are spending a great deal of time and energy worrying about how they will respond to the next incident. What will they do the next time a child fights, swears, or lies? What will they do if a child defies them and refuses to do what he or she has been told to do? There are so many "what ifs" that entire books have been produced which give solutions to various discipline problems. Unfortunately, the best solution of all is the one that is rarely mentioned.

> *Today's popular discipline is reactive*
> *and relies on intervention.*
> *Real discipline is proactive*
> *and relies on prevention.*

There are few great solutions to problems after they have occurred. Certainly, there will always be problems that must be solved. No system of discipline could possibly exert that much control. Neither would such a system be desirable. Nonetheless, nothing is gained by paying undue attention to this part of discipline. Every minute that is spent preventing problems saves many minutes when it comes to intervening after the fact.

One of the best examples of the difference between today's discipline and real discipline is the proliferation of conflict *resolution* programs in schools. Countless dollars have been spent on these programs and they often absorb a significant amount of school time. But what happened to conflict *prevention* programs? Why hasn't the market been flooded with this type of material?

Well, now you know and this forms the eleventh secret of discipline:

Prevention is the best solution.

Once a problem happens, it's history. It certainly needs to be resolved if possible, but nothing can change the fact that the incident occurred. Plus, as we all know, the incident itself is disruptive and the problem-solving process takes time. Both of these play havoc with your plans, especially when children always seem to misbehave when you are busy and don't have any time to deal with it.

So think prevention!

Here are a few ideas that will help you:

"Sponge" Activities

There is no doubt, as the old saying goes, that "idle hands are the devil's workshop". Children who have nothing appropriate to do very quickly find something inappropriate to do. So it's a good idea to provide all sorts of "sponge" activities, so called because they soak up a child's idle time.

One thing that you notice about well-run classrooms is that the students are never stuck for something to do. There are word searches, puzzles and mazes, books to be read, extra projects to be worked on, and an assortment of learning games.

Sponge activities are particularly useful for parents when they take their children on car trips. Rather than make deals with the children, promising to give them something for being good in the car, spend some time making a "trip box".

This is a box full of games, activities, books and magazines. It can only be opened and used on trips. The rest of the time, the box is kept hidden away on a shelf. Because all the activities stay fresh, children stay interested, and busy, for hours. Some good ideas for trip boxes include puzzle books, word searches, travel games, magazines, battery-operated games, and coloring materials.

Pre-Planning

Impulsive children consistently have difficulties when they head into unstructured situations such as school playgrounds. It can take years to teach them the problem-solving and decision-making skills required to handle these complex situations. In the meantime, help impulsive children do the one thing that will offset some of their impulsivity ⇨*plan*. When they go out onto the playground, insist they decide ahead of time:

    a) what game they will play,
    b) who with,
    c) where, and
    d) who has the equipment.

Parents can do the same kind of planning for trips to the shopping mall or visits with friends and relatives.

Transitions

Many problems arise when children are required to stop one activity and move to another, especially if the second activity is less desirable. You will get much less resistance if you take the time to forewarn your children that a change is coming. A "two minutes left" warning allows them to plan ahead and lowers their sense of frustration.

If cleaning up is required, lend a hand whenever possible. After all, the children didn't decide to end the activity. Under such circumstances, they appreciate a little help in putting away any toys and materials.

Make the transition as smooth as possible. The longer it takes, the more likely it is that you will be dealing with misbehavior. When you watch great teachers and parents in action, one thing that is very noticeable is that they run "snappy" transitions.

"May I?"

Many parents and teachers perceive courtesy as desirable but do not demand it from children. They think of it as an optional extra.

Don't underestimate the power of words, however. They have the ability to change the way our world works. Courtesy is important because it communicates a willingness to work co-operatively with others. At the same time, it communicates respect for the rights and needs of others. Most of us respond with obvious pleasure and appreciation to acts of courtesy, all of which helps to change the atmosphere in our homes and workplaces.

When it comes to the power of words, don't underestimate the phrase, "May I?". Adults rarely require children to speak consistently in this manner. It is important to understand, however, that the use of this phrase is a recognition of authority. In effect, the child is saying, "I know that you are in charge around here and that I need your permission to do certain things." It is very difficult for a child to ask permission and, at the same time, be in a power struggle with someone. So, if you want to avoid the arguments about who makes the final decision, start insisting on the use of these two great words.

Trouble Paying Attention?

More and more children are having difficulty keeping their minds on their work. Part of this problem is undoubtedly due to the hectic pace of the modern world, a pace that makes sustained attention difficult even for adults. In addition, children are receiving most of their information in short chunks of highly visual material. "Sesame Street" is a good example. Even advertisements have been shortened to appeal to today's short attention span. Have you noticed that some television commercials are now being repeated within a single set of commercials, just in case you weren't paying attention the first time?

For children who struggle to stay on task, try sitting them next to someone who is a natural stick-to-it person. Also try "chunking" their work, breaking it into smaller units that should only take about 5-10 minutes. Set a timer and see how much work the child can accomplish within a specific period of time (the challenge gives them a bit of extra motivation). And always remember to get their attention before giving instructions. You might even want to have the instructions repeated back to you, just to make sure that the information didn't go in one ear and out the other.

Stop Activities *Before* Problems Start

Think of this as the M*A*S*H* rule. Everyone remembers the television show M*A*S*H* which had a phenomenal run for a number of years. The cast and producers decided to end the show when it was still at the top of the ratings, a move which surprised a great many people. However, they didn't want to experience the slow death that many shows go through as they gradually slip farther and farther down the ratings scale until no one even notices when the show is finally pulled.

All too often, we fall into this same trap with our children. We extend their activities until problems arise. Then we are forced to deal with problems that could have been avoided. This happens most frequently on excursions to malls, visits to friends and general sightseeing. It also happens when children are busy playing their own games. A game is allowed to continue until there is a disagreement and then the game is stopped as a way of punishing the children for their problem.

Activities should be stopped when there are no problems at all. Most adults can sense when children are becoming irritable and overtired. When the first signs appear, alter your schedule so that the activity ends within a few minutes. This way, your excursions can stay at the top of the ratings, just like M*A*S*H*.

17

Problem Solvers

No matter how much you work at preventing problems, you will still have to deal with a significant number. Even if you limit children to the choices that are theirs to make, they are certain to make mistakes. It's part of life and it's part of growing up. Throughout this book, you have discovered a variety of new and different responses to problems from "shared rewards" to "batting practice". Here are a few more ideas for dealing with some of the most common situations faced by parents and teachers.

Lying and Stealing

Most parents and teachers express great frustration when dealing with children who lie and steal. Since the behavior is self-rewarding, any punishments may quickly become excessive. That leads to the frequent use of threats with little chance of follow-through. The following is more effective but it's also more difficult and time consuming.

Lying and stealing are a breach of trust. A child only learns the value of trust if you respond accordingly. Whenever the child wants to go somewhere or do something that involves trust, insist that he or she be supervised. There is trust in most situations, even going to the washroom (medicine cabinets or the opportunity to throw water). The

Judge, Jury, and Referee

How many times has this happened to
you? You have a boy in front of you who
probably did something wrong. He denies
it. You present the facts as you see them.
He says you can't prove it. You question other children who
may have witnessed the event. Then you present all the
evidence. More denials. The other children are lying, he claims.
Now, you're trapped. You're certain he's the culprit but, just to
be on the safe side, you decide not to punish him. After all,
what if he is telling the truth? He would probably hate you
forever. Well, here is a different point of view.

Millions of television viewers watched Judge Wapner preside
over a variety of cases. One day, he had to deal with a
particularly difficult situation. Both sides had good evidence
and presented strong arguments. Finally, he made his decision.
Later, a student in the audience asked, "With such difficult
cases, how can you be sure you made the right decision?"

"Oh, it's not my job to be right every time," replied the judge.
"To do that, I would need hundreds of detectives to search for
evidence. Even then, it would be very difficult. My job is to
listen to all the evidence, assess the credibility of the plaintiffs
and then make my best judgment. That's my job. I'm a judge.
Hopefully, I'm right most of the time but I don't lose sleep
over it."

So listen to children, take their credibility into account, and
then make your call. Don't worry so much about being perfect.
Just use your best judgment. What's good for a judge is good
for parents and teachers.

child must wait for supervision or, if none is available, miss the activity.

But, here's the key. This must be done in the matter-of-fact manner of an instructor. You are teaching the child the value of trust, **not** punishing the child by removing privileges and making life inconvenient. Simply explain that people who can't be trusted must be supervised. Someone must be with them to make sure they behave correctly.

Most children quickly become exasperated with this situation. They begin asking to do things on their own. This is now a teaching situation. Allow them small bits of freedom at first. If they handle themselves correctly, then gradually give more and more. Now they will understand the value of trust.

If the behavior is repeated, you may need to add in a punishment to give the child a very clear message that "No means No!". Just don't rely on punishment as your only response or the child will become sneakier rather than more responsible.

Remember!

Ask your child, "Would you have done the same thing if I had been standing next to you?"

When the child responds "No", then your next question is:

"Why do you need me standing next to you for you to make a good choice?".

School Homework

If teachers ever wanted to seek revenge on parents, all they would have to do is assign more homework. Just saying that word is enough to send shivers up the backs of many parents.

Everyone knows that homework is important. After all, it's clearly impossible for children to prepare themselves for the modern world in just five hours each school day. But, how do you get kids to do their homework without a battle?

The first step is to understand the roles. When teachers assign work, it's their job to check for accuracy and completion. Parents are responsible for creating a structure in the home environment which promotes the completion of homework. This requires the provision of an appropriate work location, supervision, and assistance as required.

When homework is not being completed, or is not being brought home, it is clear that the student does not care enough about the homework. Therefore, the decision-making transfers to the adults. At home, the parents should decide on a minimum amount  of time which will be set aside each day for learning, whether or not work is brought home from school. If the child claims that there is no homework, then the time is used for reading, studying or working ahead on projects.

For teachers, once homework is assigned, don't allow students to disregard their assignments or they will disregard other teacher instructions and directions as well. Don't use the threat of low marks to bargain for compliance because this technique only works with the students who are already completing their homework. The only real question should be **when** the homework will be completed, **not whether**. It is important that this perspective be instilled in students right from the primary grades. Once the students are taller than the teacher, it is too late.

Disputes

Small disputes are a common part in the daily lives of children. All too often, adults attempt to referee these spats and end up frustrated and exasperated. When children are very young (under the age of four), adult intervention is often necessary, although it should be done with a minimum of discussion.

By the age of five, most children are quite capable of resolving their own disputes. Try the following sequence whenever children have a conflict which is big enough to require your attention. Start by assigning them to a discussion area such as the kitchen table. Tell them that they must remain there until they work out their problem.

When they do, they come to you and each must tell you that the problem has been solved. Resist the temptation to ask what solution they came up with. Often, children will reach an understanding that is not easy to explain. Besides, the details of the solution are rarely important.

There is a good reason why each child must tell you that the problem has been solved. Often, one child will attempt to coerce the other with some sort of threat: "If you don't tell Mom that this problem is solved, I'm going to break your favorite toy!" You can usually tell when this has occurred. The child who has taken control will usually be the first to tell you that the problem has been solved, so it's important to hear it from the other child as well. Chances are, they will use a different tone of voice and different words. You will hear a very passive, uncertain voice saying, "Yes, I guess it was solved." Tell the first child that you know exactly what occurred, disallow it, and send them back to finish their job. It is under these circumstances that you may have to monitor the situation and request the details of the resolution.

Remember that children must be taught the skills for handling these problem-solving situations. They don't learn them by accident. Sit with them during the first few times that they are discussing a conflict and teach them exactly what you want them to do. In fact, you may wish to practice the skills ahead of time, before there is an incident. That will decrease the stress for everyone.

Temper Tantrums

Very young children occasionally have temper tantrums because they cannot get what they want, feel frustrated, and are unable to communicate. By the age of four, however, such tantrums should be a thing of the past. If you have a child who is continuing to show this behavior, it is likely because the child has learned to use the tantrums as a weapon. The longer they carry on the yelling and screaming, the more likely you are to give in. This is "behavior management" in reverse, where the child is using punishment to manage you.

The simple rule about temper tantrums is to never give in. Never! Now, if you need to say something to the child, try, "This doesn't work on me." Then repeat your previous direction. For instance, if you had previously told the child to put away a toy, then simply say it again. This is called the "broken record" technique. Don't give new information. Avoid making deals or threatening punishments. If you offer up deals at this point, they will have more temper tantrums in the future in order to see what new deals might come their way.

In the future, make it clear to your children that you are always willing to reconsider an issue if they speak politely. If they have a temper tantrum, however, there will be no discussion and no reconsideration. Call it the "temper tantrum guarantee". The moment the tantrum begins, you guarantee that the child will not get whatever is being demanded.

Interruptions

Young children interrupt because whatever is on their mind is the most important issue in the world at that moment. They are absolutely convinced that you must be just as concerned about it as they are. At this age, they must be taught when interruptions are appropriate and when they are considered rude.

For older children who should know better, the key is to respond with a signal such as holding out your hand in a typical "Stop" motion. However, do not respond either with your voice or your eyes. The latter part of this is particularly difficult and must be practiced.

This is important because, in our culture, we use both our voices and our eyes to start conversations. If you turn and speak to children when they interrupt, they will start to say whatever is on their mind. But if you turn and make eye contact with them, that starts them talking as well. A "Stop" hand signal is the most effective response. Then, at the right time, remember to ask them what they wanted to say.

Teasing

Most parents and teachers are a bit mystified when it comes to dealing with teasing. After all, we do quite a bit of it ourselves, teasing both our children and our friends. Usually, it is considered humorous and a sign of affection or friendship.

When a child teases, however, it often hurts the feelings of another child. How can children be taught the right way to tease someone else? Should they be punished for hurting someone's feelings?

It is best to think of teasing in three ways and deal with each differently:

Friendly teasing, which is good natured and should be laughed at by both the giver and the receiver. If a child overreacts to this type of teasing, help him or her recognize that no spite was intended. It's important for children to learn to laugh at themselves.

Incidental teasing, which may have gone a little too far but wasn't intended to hurt. Teach the child on the receiving end to ignore this type of teasing or to make a statement such as, "Please stop teasing me." If the teasing continues, teach the first child that he or she has gone too far. You may need to teach this many times, since each situation is different. Remember that the limits on teasing are very abstract and difficult to learn. Children need many teaching messages in many different situations.

Aggressive teasing is intended to hurt the other person and should be dealt with as verbal "hit". Respond with the same clear statement of limits that you use for physical hits. Consider having a "No put-downs!" rule in your home or classroom. Use this phrase whenever you hear the kind of aggressive teasing that is supposed to make someone feel small. Be prepared to enforce your rules. No means no!

Fighting

When you are called upon to break up a fight, resist the temptation to resolve the issues immediately. Emotions are usually much too intense and the children will simply continue to bicker. Separate them and allow some cooling-off time.

As with other disputes, it is often possible for the participants to resolve the issues that led to their fight. However, you may need to supervise the discussion to ensure that another fight does not begin.

Note that most fights begin with verbal hits. In the future, watch for these and attempt to stop violence at this early level. As verbal sparring begins, consider using words, "Don't hit." Children are often surprised at this choice of words and will respond, "I didn't touch him." You are then in a position to make the concept of verbal hits clear and to disallow them. It is a much more powerful way of dealing with the issue.

When you are called upon to deal with a fight, also deal seriously with any spectators who eagerly supported the conflict. They are involved in the fight just as much as the actual participants. Peer pressure is very important. Spectators should be stopping a fight, not aggravating the situation.

"All Aboard"

A few years from now, our children will be in charge of our country and our communities. They will decide how senior citizens (That's us!) will be treated. They will be responsible for looking after the environment, preventing wars, and educating a new generation of children. How well our children do in the years to come will, to a great extent, be determined by how well we raise them now. This is why discipline should never be equated with punishment. It has far more to do with education and maturity, cooperation and values.

So climb aboard. Let's start moving back to real discipline, to teaching our children the skills and attitudes they need for the modern world. Let's teach them to be responsible, cooperative and productive. Let's teach them respect for rules, for authority, and for the rights and needs of others. It won't be easy. Before you start, understand the commitment that you will have to make. Time is only the first part.

It Takes Time to Move a Mountain

We live in a very busy world. There is never enough time to accomplish all the things we want to do. That is one of the reasons why rewards and consequences became so popular. They are quick and easy. In a world full of fast food and instant communication, today's discipline fits right in. It may not do the job, but it's convenient.

Real discipline isn't. It takes time to supervise children. It takes time to instruct them and direct their actions. It takes time to build positive relationships. There is no way around it. When you read in chapter 11 about the importance of rehearsal and positive practice, you probably said something to yourself like, "Sounds good but where in the world would anyone get the time to do it?"

Remember that one of the lessons you are trying to teach your children is to put what needs to be done ahead of what they feel like doing. So be prepared to miss some of your favourite television shows. It takes longer than a commercial break to put children to bed in a caring and loving manner.

Be prepared to get up off the couch, out of the garage, away from your desk and out of the kitchen. If you try to discipline from where you are, you will use words instead of actions, threats instead of authority. Compliance training requires direct supervision.

So if real discipline is what you want for your children, then set aside the time that real discipline takes. There is no other way.

Take Charge

Next, you must make a commitment to authority. You must be willing to take charge of your children, to make the decisions that need to be made, and to impose the limits that are an essential part of real discipline.

This is not easy. It is the exact opposite of what you have been told to do over the past 15 to 20 years. Throughout that time period, parents and teachers were told to bargain for compliance. Deal-making and pleading replaced the use of natural authority. Leadership all but disappeared. It's no surprise that children lost respect for their parents and teachers.

We have spent far too long treating our children like miniature adults. We've tried to befriend them, treat them like equals, have them vote on decisions, and make them happy. We thought they would appreciate our efforts and respond in kind.

Forget it. It doesn't work.

Homes and classrooms are not democracies where children have an equal voice in decision-making. It isn't their job to make up rules. That responsibility belongs to parents and teachers.

We have a job to do, an important job. Whether children like our decisions or not is irrelevant. Whether they agree with us or not is irrelevant. Discipline is not a popularity contest. The important issue is that children respect our decisions, and there is no respect where there is no authority.

Insist on Growth

Finally, you must be committed to the concept that children should behave better as they grow older. This may sound obvious at first but it is important to understand that today's popular discipline has affected everyone's expectations, including yours.

By allowing children to make their own decisions, today's discipline gives children the option of behaving *less* responsibly as they get older, as long as they are willing to accept the consequences of their actions.

This is why many children are more courteous as eight-year-olds than they are as teenagers, despite the fact that courtesy is a skill which should improve over time. Rude behavior from adolescents has now become so commonplace that many adults consider it a natural phase. This is nonsense. Teenagers do not suddenly acquire a rudeness hormone. Nor is antagonistic behavior a natural part of the maturation process. Children are entirely capable of developing independence and being polite at the same time, but only if you accept nothing less.

Look at discipline, not as an event, but as a process. Most incidents are not very important. Deal with them and get on with real discipline. Teach your children to do better tomorrow than they did today. This is the issue of continuous progress. As long as children behave better each day, then they will eventually learn to behave responsibly and co-operatively. Your natural instincts support this kind of growth. It's why you look at an eight-year-old who's having a temper tantrum and say, "Don't behave like a four-year-old."

When parents and teachers view discipline in this way, they stop trying to get agreement on rewards and consequences. Instead, they agree on the kind of child they want a certain child to become. They discuss what skills the child needs to learn and who will do the teaching. From then on, they communicate about the child's progress, not about mistakes. When adults undertake real discipline, they share insights, not incidents.

Now you understand the commitment that real discipline requires. You have to decide for yourself if you are prepared to make the investment. Just remember - there are no shortcuts. This is the twelfth secret of discipline:

There is no great discipline without great commitment.

Getting Started

Let's say that you are willing to make the commitment that is required for real discipline. How will you know where to start? The best "rule of thumb" is to start small. Too many people try to change everything all at once. It can't be done. When they fail, they get frustrated and return to old ways of doing discipline. Try not to fall into this trap. Just change a few small things at first. Add more later when you're ready.

Here are a few starting points:

▸ Try "do-overs". When your children are rude, stop them and insist that they start over. If they run down a flight of stairs, send them back to walk.

▸ Decide which one of their chores has been causing you the most irritation and supervise its completion. When you give directions, start with small items. Remember to set the stage by providing food, music or other enjoyable items.

▸ Teach your children a new behavior that they will need in the near future. If you are a parent, consider improving the way that your children answer the phone and take messages. For teachers, consider taking your class to the auditorium and honing their assembly skills.

Three-Part Harmony

As you undertake this huge task of raising and teaching children, remember to balance the three parts of discipline. They need to be well-trained so they will work well within the structure that society requires. They need to be well-taught so they have the skills and attitudes for being responsible and co-operative. They also need to have choices so they learn how to handle independence.

Remember that good training and good teaching form the foundation of real discipline. Children should only be given choices when they are ready to handle them.

This is especially true for all the children who struggle with today's discipline, those who are impulsive, abused, or neglected. We have to do more for these children. Today's discipline gives them the option of drifting from failure to failure, punishment to punishment. They need more. They need real discipline, as do all our children.

This is the challenge that I leave with you. It's time to get discipline back on track. It's time to return to real discipline. The future of our children and our communities depends upon it.

Secrets of Discipline

Never give a choice
When it comes to limits.

If you bargain for compliance now,
You'll beg for it later.

When children are well-trained,
It's habit-forming.

Rules worth having,
Are worth enforcing.

Behavior that needs to be learned,
Needs to be taught.

Today's practice is
Tomorrow's performance.

(Continued)

Secrets of Discipline

(continued)

Independence isn't 'doing your own thing';
It's doing what's right on your own.

Keep responsible decisions,
In responsible hands.

Discipline comes best from the heart,
Not the hand.

Beware of self-indulgence,
Disguised as self-esteem.

Prevention is the best solution

There is no great discipline,
Without great commitment.

If you liked the book,
You'll love the video.

SECRETS OF DISCIPLINE
for raising responsible children

Secrets of Discipline is also available as a video presentation. This 80 minute performance, filmed in front of a live audience, will provide you with a host of fresh insights.

To receive up-to-date information about ordering the video or additional copies of this book, send a completed copy of the following form to Woodstream Publishing, P.O. Box 1093, Fonthill, Ontario, Canada L0S 1E0.

For a speedier reply, fax the form to (905) 892-8936.

I wish to receive up-to-date information for ordering the Secrets of Discipline video and/or additional copies of the book. Also include updates regarding new materials. Please send the information to:

Name:_____

Organization:_____

Address:_____

City:_____ Prov/State:_____ Code:_____

Phone:_____ Fax:_____

Send to: Woodstream Publishing, P.O. Box 1093, Fonthill, Ontario, Canada L0S 1E0
Or fax to: (905) 892-8936